LEARNING HUMAN BEHAVIOR HOW INFLUENCES ECONOMY DEVELOPMENT

JOHN LOK

Contents

Preface

Introduction

Nowadays, we are experiencing new economic development period. Many countries societies will have significant unpredicted change, however, we will difficult to predict whether what our societies will change or how and why we future societies will have these possible changes. I write this book aims to explain whether what some social changes will be causes to influence our daily living in possible future development. Due to we are experiencing new economic development period, so we ought to attempt to predict whether what our societies will be influenced to change by new economic development.

What are our social customer and economic problems ususally we will encounter in our live? Human behavior or technology influence economy development? Can economists apply any economic theories to attempt to solve any economic or customer problems absolutely? Do economists apply any economic theories to solve any problems in any economic environment or suitations or they need find the suitable economic theories to solve the suitable environment of economic or customer problems? I shall attempt to apply new economy theory to explain below industries how develops to change in order to achieve customer purchase or entertinment desire to their products or entertainment service.

Readers can make analysis whether any above issues occur how to influence our future social development to be improved better or worse. I hope my readers can judge new economic society whether is better to compare traditional old economic society or worse to compare traditional old economic society. Our technology will assist our society to develop or it can bring negative impact to influence our future social development. Readers can have more clear answers after you read this book.

Prologue

manufacturer sale number in recession period
● How to develop organizations in growth stage?
● How to apply business development strategy to help educational robotic manufacturers to enter traditional education market ?
● Future educational robotic are applied on development teaching maths market
    Learning behavioral economy to solve social challenges
● Why do some social challenges may influence customers number ?
Organizational life cycle stage decision making strategy
● Why do managers feel difficult to make
decisions?
    Computer technological firm merger cooperational strategy
● IBM and Apple merger strategic advantages and
disadvantages

Chapter 3
Technology or human behavior influences economy development

Human Behavioral network job brings social
economic benefits p.51-65
    What does human network job mean
    Why human network job behavior may influence economy

Robots take our jobs behavioral and economy influences
    Robot job behavior brings economy influences

Intellectual human economic behaviors p.66-80
What does intellectual human economic behaviors
mean ?
    The relationship between social change and human
behavior
    How human productive behavior may influence economic development

● New Zealand farmer individual wine productive behavior
● America high technological productive behavior
● China share market investing behavior
Why has any individual country have many people invest share behavior which can influence the country's macro consumption desire?

Can technology influence human shopping behavioral change?

Why and how human behavior may influence the country's economic growth or recession?

Technology how impacts human behavior changing?

How and why employees behaviors may influence economy development?

Robots invention whether they can help organizations to raise efficiencies or inefficiencies? p.81-99

Why social behavior may influence organizational strategy needs to be changed ?

Reasons why human behavior may influence economic recession or growth ?

How employee behavior influences organizational development?

Artificial intelligent Human clever and art creating ability methods

Why does technology raise online products sale demand and reduces shops products sale demand?

Does car technological development reach mature stage to help economic development?

CHAPTER ONE

Electronic vehicle and non -manual driven vehicle invention how to bring negative impact to passengers' public transport needs

Nowadays, since electronic vehicle invention, it brought competition to fight traditional gas vehicle martet. Electronic vehicle is only needed to be charged battery, then battery will bring energy to push the electornic car to be driven fastly. So traditional vehicle market is experiencing decline life cycle stage. When, electronic vehicle is popular to be accepted to every drivers. In fact, when we drive cars on the roads, our cars will have gas emission to polluate our sir. Earth warmth is dramatically increasing. The main reason is that global air is polluted, e.g. frequent driving activities will bring air pollution when gas emission is caused. Hecnce, environment vehicle is only needed to charged battery. Every time battery charged can bring one day driving time power or enerty to let drivers to drive . So, basing on environmental protection and battery long time driving both reasons, it brings strengths to electronic vehicle to persuade global any drivers to choose to buy electronic vehicle more than traditional gas vehicle. I shall research these questions: These questions may concern: Will the gas vehicle be influenced to experience the decline life cycle stage rapidly when the electronic vehicle is accepted to be popular to drive ? Can traditional gas vehicle avoid decline life cycle stage comes as well as if traditional gas vehicle real prepares to experience decline life cycle stage ? Can it re-grow to change to enter growth life cycle stage again? Can new electronic vehicle market influence traditional gas vehicle market to shorten time to experience decline life cycle age rapidly?

In our driving history, cars invention had helped us do not need to spend long walking time to go to anywhere conveniently. In fact, due to technological limit, e.g. bus, taxi, tram, train must use gas to be energy to push them to be driven on the roads. When car invention period, or it may call car market birth life cycle stage period. In the 1800 year beginning , human does not know what car function or why we need car. When cars had been invented, it is global whole car industry borth life cycle stage period. This period its characteristics are: In societies , people accepted car tools to drive on the roads. Many people feel to spend money to buy cars, it is waste money, because they may choose to catch any kinds of public transport tools, e.g. bus, train, tram, taxi, ferry, undergroundtrain to arrive any destinations conveniently. So, from 1800 year to 1900 year, global whole car industy had been still keeping in the growth life cycle stage. Because in global society, many people hasd been general accepting public tranposrt tools, their fee are vey cheap and passengers can spend short time to catch them to go to anywhere, they can provide long transport service time for office working people, student from morning to evening time. Hence, this 100 years period, global car sale number could not significant increase, because public transport tools could bring convenience to any one when they needed to leave homes to arrive far away destination in short time.

Hence, global car industry ought not develop rapidly, because many people could not accept to spend money to buy cars to replace to catch any public transport tools. But after 1900 year, global whole gas vehicle industry began to experience growth life cycle stage. Because global many people had jobs to do, unemployment ratio begain to reduce. In society, rich people number began to increase. It based on theseboth factors: families began to consider to attempt to buy any kinds of cars in order to attempt to buy any kinds of cars in order to let them to feel enjoyable to drive to go to anywhere. So, from 1901 year to 2000 year, it may be global whole gas vehicle market growth life cycle stage . In this period, global car buyers number had been increasing significantly . In average, global every family may own at least one car, even more. It depends on whether how many members number, the family has and whether the family has how many member(s), he/she has own one car licence. Moreover, in society, many people began to accept second hand cars, because second hand cars must be chaper to compare new cars as well as it is real one good choice for the low income car buyer social consumer groups in society. So, in this global vehicle market growth life cycle stage, instead of new car buyers number had been increasing significantly, the second hand car buyers number had also been increasing significantly in the same time. So, global new cars and secod hand car buyers number had increased rapidly every year, because global population is increasing. It also caused many working people did not like to spend long time to queue to wait public transport tools, it is another factor to persuade people chooce to buy cars to drive to go to offices or schools or anywhere in their relax time, e.g. holiday, sunday. So, this 100 year, may be global whole car industry growth life car cycle stage.

After 2000, it may be global car industy mature life cycle ctage , many car manufacturers begun to innovate any kinds of traditional cars to change to advanced engine function, auto-window, auto dooe functions , navigation road locaion search function, even non-manual driven artificial intelligent car invention. So, after 2000 year, due to global car buyers begun to pursue comfortable drivin feeling. They need to pursue comfortable driving feeling. They need to buy unique design of cars, or more functions of cars to drive on the road . Hence, global different unique function and styles of cars purchase needs had been significant increasing. Moreover, car prices had also been increasing more, due to more different unique functional and styles of car purchase needs had been increasing in order to satisfy the rich or high income car buyers group. So, after 2000, it may be global car market 's mature life cycle stage.

But, I believe that global car market's mature life cycle stage can not keep long time. The main reason is because the electronic car invention. After 2000 year, since one kind of new transport tool of electronic car invention, it influences many gas car owners or non car owners feel interesting to learn how to drive electronic cars and feel whether what advantages that electronic cars can satisfy their driving needs. IN special, environmental protection awareness drivers must believe electornic cars can reduce air pollution when they choose to drive them on the roads , due to none gas emission effect to pollute our earth air. When they choose to drive electronic cars, due to they only need to charge battery, then their electronic cars can be driven on the roads in short time rapidly. Even, report also indicated driving electronic cars accident occurrence chance may be also influenced to reduce to compare driving gas cars usually. So, electronic vehicle market may be future main competitor to global traditional gas vehicle market.

May electronic vehicle invention influence future gas vehicle shorten time to experience to decline life cycle stage rapidly? How gas vehicle market may avoid the shorten time to experience decline life cycle stage if electronic vehicle market may influence its development in global car manufacture industry? I shall attempt to solve these challenges as below:

IN fact, electronic vehicle innovation is not long time , so the global electronic vehicle manufacturing and sale market is experiencing birth life cycle stage. Can electronic vehicle market reduce to shorten time to experience growth, even mature life cycle stages. It depends on these factors:

The factors may affect battery electronic vehicle energy consumption and driving behavior impact. They may include whether environment protection awareness will increase or decrease to global nay one gas car owners or non car owners. Because if global environment protection awareness increase, it will influence gas car owners or non car owners (potential either battery electronic vehicle energy or gas vehicle energy car choice buyers), begun to feel their frequent driving gas vehicle behaviors may bring air pollution or global warming, temperature rises weather disaster occurrence in the future. They alsoknow battery electronic vehicle energy consumption price may be cheap to same to gas vehicle energy consumption. Moreover, they may feel that if they change to drive battery electronic vehicles, it may help them to minimize environmental air pollution impacts of the end of life stage and brings positive impacts on improving climate change and air quality for our future. So, if many car owners or non car owners feel that they have responsibility to protect our climate environment pollution. Then, battery electronic vehicle buyers number will have possible to increase rapidly in short time. Due to the significant impact of gas vehicle and battery electronic vehicle their life cycle analysis can be utilized to analyze the advantages and disadvantages to cause car buyers make comparison between them and gas vehcile and battery electronic vehcile both kinds vehicles are highly complex supply chain choice in the automobile industry nowadays. Moreover, due to carbon intensity of this stage was calculated from emission factors at the global car manufacture industry. Hence, emission factor may be one important influential factor to influence any one makes car purchase decision or either gas or battery electronic car purchase decison.

For example , in our societies, if many people own environment protection awareness, then global gas vehicle buyers number may be influenced to reduce, even the owning gas vehicle families may be influenced to choose to buy battery electronic cars to replace their gas cars. They may sell their gas vehicles to any one, even to steel manufacturers easily. Hence, gas vehicle on steel existence number may also reduce ot they can disappear in our road in short time rapidly. If batttery electronic vehcile can be popular to accept to drive on the road to any one driver in our societies. Then, battery electronic cars may be influenced to increase driving needs to any one driver. it's sale number may also influenced to increase rapidly. Consequently, it may have chance to experience to growth life cycle stage from birth life cycle stage in short time rapidly in global whole electronic car manufacturer and sale market.

Then another influential factor concerns how owning car consumers feel the charge of the battery energy use of resources in comparison to conventional gas energy use of resources to driving cars. In combination with the regional electricity mix these factors influence the energy materials for a specific car market. For these first life cycle phases a range of values is possible to battery electronic car market. If in our societies, there are many people choose to use battery charge energy resource to drive electronic cars, their prices are very reasonable to compare gas vehicles or they feel gas will face rapid shortage challenge, if global any one only likes to drive gas vehicle. Then, they may be influenced to choose to buy the battery electronic vehicles to replace gas vehicles. Hence, enery resource used to car my also be one main factor to influence any one car buyer individual either battery electronic car or gas vehicle purchase choice.

Hence, it implies that the life style environmental impacts and energy resource used both impacts of battery electronic cars are a topic of increasing relative importance of the vehicle production stage and the maximum impact on climate change (ingc02/km) that is observed by many climate scientists, their observation to climate change good or bad change effect may influence global battery electronic vehicle needs. So, how clean are battery electric cars, it will be one popular topic for environmental scientists to environmental protection awareness car owners and non car owners. T o analysis hoe to cause electric car life cycle changes. The arrival of the electric car has brought with it an array of life cycle factors that influence the carbon emission level to any one country's environment.

Influence of national electricity grid over the use phase, so it implies that if the country feels carbon emission level is high , due to gas vehicle may bring carbon emission to pollute air to the country. Although, factory's carbon emission or airplane carbon emisson may be one factor to influence the country's air pollution level to be increase. The year has high carbon emission level, it considers gas vehicle air carbon emission level whether it is high or low in the year. So, if the country's gas vehicle car owners number is sudden increasing rapidly. Consequently, it will evaluate that the car increasing number may influence the country itself carbon emission level to be high and it may cause air pollution seriously.

Hence, battery electric car industry life cycle whether when it can experience growth life cycle stage or mature life cycle stage from birth life cycle stage, it depends on what carbon emisson level to any one country. If this year has many countries believe their high carbon emissin level is due to gas vehicle 's carbon emission causes. Then, this high carbon emission level report factor may raise many car owners or non car owners consider environment protection awareness and it may also influence many car buyers choose to buy battery electric cars to replace gas cars to drive on the road frequently in this year.

Also in order to avoid themselves countries' air pollution is more serious. Hence, global carbon emission rise or fall level and any one environmental protection awareness psychological both factors may influence future battery electric car market development. They may have close relationship to influence any one traditional gas vehicle owner to buy one new battery vehicle vehicle to replace it to drive on the road, or any one potential car purchaser makes final battery electric car or gas vehicle decision absolutely. On conclusion, above these factors may explain whether it is possible that battery electronic vehicle invention may influence future gas vehicle market changes to decline life cysle stage from mature life cycle stage. It depends on whether environmental protection awareness to car owners increasing or decreasing number , carbon emission level whether it is high or low, gas energy resource facing shortage factors to influence future electronic vehicle need.

● Electronic vehicle invention causes future underground train transportation needs to know passenger behaviour reasons

Understanding individual passenger behaviour is essential for the design MTR transportation, because who can choose to catch bus, taxi, tram, train ferry etc. different kinds of public transportation tools. Individual traveler who decides to catch which kinds of public transportation tools, it depends on whether the public transportation tool can provide real time travel information, liking link travel time schedule. So, MTR underground train needs to understand where it has terminal to give convenience to the local living areas of time travelers to choose to catch MTR easily. Although, MTR ticket fare is one factor to influence any passengers choice. But, those other factors can also influence them to choice. e.g. MTR any terminal location of convenience, short time travelling, none crowding in busy (peak) time, MTR platform waiting arrival time, none sudden MTR engineering machines broken accident events occurrence frequently etc. different factors, any one of these factors which can influence passengers who choose to catch MTR or other kinds of transportation tools.

Why route choice can influence passenger behavioural choice ? Usually, the busy time passengers will regard the route choice as a coordination problem to influence them to choose to catch which kinds of transportation tools. The route choice is as an opportunity costs to influence any busy time passengers to decide to choose to catch which kind of transportation tool which is the best right choice in the right time among of them. In the short time, for example, it seems any busy time passengers will choose to catch bus to substitute MTR underground train transportation tool, due to who feels the bus can arrive any destinations to compare other kinds of transportation tools in the most short time. However even if the MTR can either charge cheaper ticket fare to sell full day or charge discount ticket fare to sell in the busy (peak) time to compare to bus fare. It is possible that the busy time passengers will still choose to catch bus, if between the bus terminal and the another bus terminal that distance is the shorter time route to spend time to arrive destination to compare between the MTR terminal to the another MTR terminal arrival time . Also, although the busy time passengers will feel to enounter traffic jam to influence sitting or waiting bus time to be longer time in possible and who also feel MTR can avoid traffic jam problem. However, usually any busy (peak) time passengers will feel the chance of traffic jam occurrence will be less. So, the short bus route choice is more potential factor to influence the busy (peak) time passengers still to choose bus to catch.

However, if anyone wants to investigate results of day-to-day route choice which can be transferred to more realistic environment. It is necessary to explore individual behaviour in an interactive experimental set up to ensure busy (peak) time passenger transportation behavioural choice. For example, a passenger has a choice between a main road (M) and a side road (S) for travelling from (A) to (B). (M) is faster if (M) and (S) are chose by the same number of passengers. So, this method can be researched whether MTR terminal station is located at the main road (M) or the side road (S) where is more suitable to accept to passengers generally.

Why trip time reliability and crowding factors can influence MTR passenger choice? Other problem is MTR busy (peak) time's crowding in public transportation occurrence of MTR underground train transportation tool is becoming a growth to concern as MTR demand growth at a busy (peak) time. To capture the MTR passengers benefits with reduced crowding from improved MTR public transport service and image. It is necessary a identify the relevant dimensions of crowding that are meaningful measures of what crowding means to MTR passengers. Two main influences on MTR model choice that are growing in relevance are trip time reliability and crowding. It represents a benefit-cost framework. In fact, MTR passengers can be willing to pay more expensive ticket fare, it MTR can avoid crowding and short and the accurate arrival trip time between terminals is reliable to occur. How to measure of MTR crowding, e.g. weighting the gap between the busy time, the standard (i.e. objective) and the perceived (i.e. subjective) metrics. We are not in a position to definitely map the two dimensions, which is a crucial requirement for translating objective improvements into equivalent subjective gains that then can be applied, willingness to pay estimates MTR ticket fares to obtain the additional MTR passenger benefits of MTR public transportation investment to any terminal stations. Because MTR crowding has a negative impact on passengers in terms of psychological on emotional distress. MTR passengers are willing to stand for up to 20 minutes of the service is fast and reliable. However crowding outweighed these benefits from a MTR passenger's perpective, experienced crowding leads a increased dissatisfaction. e.g. stress and less privacy during who needs to stand up in MTR. Due to there are no enough places to supply to them to stand up in MTR. If the MTR trip time was longer time between the passenger's terminals, who will feel more dissatisfaction and it will cause who feels whether who ought need to choose to catch other transportation tools to substitute MTR next time. e.g. bus, train, tram, ferry, taxi etc. So, from an operator's perspective, the MTR service frequency or MTR size is significantly influenced by the level of ridership, which sends a signal to respond if the monitored crowding level exceeds the benchmark standard in the busy time. e.g. in the morning time or at the night time, the students or employment people who need to go to schools or offices (working places). The locations of different places between MTR terminals and crowding are regarded as a key service attribute for MTR pubic transportation along with other factors, such as travelling time and reliability, e.g. service quality, none engineering machines are broken to cause MTR stops suddenly.

Given the increasing importance of crowding on both the disutility to existing MTR public transportation users and the influence to it. MTR passenger can choose to use either the MTR public public transportation or other public transportation. It is timely to review the MTR current measures of crowding defined by transportation authorities. MTR operators ought evaluate whether they apporpriately reflect MTR each traveler experiences and perceptions of crowding in busy (peak) time. I suggest that MTR needs to buy other underground trains to supply to the busy (peak) time passengers to let them have enough seats to sit down, so who do not need to stand up in any MTR underground trains when they catch MTR underground trains in busy time. It aims to let who are willingness to pay the estimation of reasonable ticket fares to compare the other kinds of transportation tools in the busy (peak) time.

What is the crowding difference between train and MTR underground train? In fact, crowding won't be happened to brother these transportation tools easily in the busy time and non busy time both. e.g. bus, taxi, train, tram, ferry. Because passengers can not choose to stand up in these transportation tools easily, due to these transportation tools have no enough areas (spaces) to let them to stand up easily . So, the crowding will be avoided to occur in these tranportation tools usually. Otherwise, MTR will have many passengers who can choose to stand up because MTR design of length is very long and it has enough areas (places) to let passengers to choose to stand up, even there have none any seats are provided to let them to sit down. So, MTR passengers will feel more dissatisfaction and crowding easily, especial in any peak (busy) time every day.

Comparing to bus, much more diverse crowding measures are defined in the passenger rail industry. For passenger, different specifications for measuring crowding are found across countries and even within a country. For example, rail crowding measures in the UK, the passengers in excess of capacity is crowding measure that applies to all London and South east operators weekday train services at a London terminus during the morning peak from 0700 to 09: 59 , and those departing during the afternoon peak from 16:00 to 18:59 (office of rail regulation 2011 year). The overall PIXC figure is considered the planned standard class capacity of each train service as well as the actual number of standard class passengers on the service at the critical point. i.e. the location on a trains of standard class passengers that surpass the planned capacity as the difference between the number of actual passengers and the capacity of the train divided by the number of passenger is within the capacity . So, it seems train and MTR underground public transportaton tools had been encountering the crowding problems in peak time, the difference in train passengers need to wait next train or more train arrival is who doesn't plan to enter the train, when who discovers the current train has no seats to provide to them to sit down in whose trip. Otherwise, MTR passengers can choose either to stand up within the large areas (places) if who discovered there are no any seats to provide to them to sit down or who can wait the next MTR arrival in order to who can sit down. It seems MTR transportation tool crowding environment includes in waiting platform and inside of the MTR underground train. Otherwise, train transportation tool crowding environment only includes the waiting platform and the passengers will not have crowding feeling inside of the train, due to none of passengers choose to stand up inside any trains because any train inside has no enough places to let them to stand up. How MTR can attract many passengers. On the commuter departure time choice of any reference point researching hand, the departure time decisions of communters are of fundamental importance of peak period MTR traffic congestion. However, whether on the demand side, MTR underground train congestion relief measures, such as MTR ticket fare to every terminal station needs to be charged cheaper fare or discount fare in the peak (busy) time every day. To aim to attract many passengers to choose to catch MTR Underground train public transportation tools, substitute to choose other public transportation tools in the peak time.

Over the past decades, there have been very active research efforts in the departure time problem, both in econometric modeling and dynamic user equilibrium fields. Although, these works provide valuable insights into dynamic commuter decision making, they do not identify the commuters' response to gains and losses related to whole actual arrival time to reference points who may have relative. The appliability of the reference point hypothesis of prospect theory to the commuter's departure time decision making to obtain a better understanding of how departure time choice in MTR platform during their waiting underground train arrival time. However, every MTR underground train actual arrival time and deviation variables related to reference points (gains and losses) are the key factors in the departure time choice model. How the MTR underground train of every commaunter's daily departure time decision can be modelled when the reference point hypothesis of prospect theory. The MTR underground train's schedule delay is defined as the difference between the preferred arrival time (PAT) and the actual arrival time (AT) for a given MTR commaunter. In a daily MTR commute, a commuter in the indifference band actual arrival time is an essential feature of MTR schedule study. Two reference points are the earliest acceptable arrival time and the work starting time for a given MTR platform waiting passengers. In psychological view point, prospect theory proposes that the displeasure of a loss is perceived or greater than the pleasure of a gain of the same attitude and therefore, the value function is stronger for losses than gains.

To conclude, it seems that if MTR waiting passengers need not spend long time to wait underground train arrival in platform and it can provide seats to let them to sit down in the busy (peak) crowding time. It will make them to feel pleasure, even the MTR ticket fare is not fair and reasonable to charge higher fare to compare other kinds of public transportation tools fares. So the peak waiting time factor can influence the passengers to choose other kind of transportation tools to catch easily. Moreover, MTR's two reference points are the earliest role. Similarly a loss is observed when the MTR platform waiting commuter experiences or actual arrival time which is beyond that the MTR schedule time. Due to that a MTR waiting commuter is as an early side arrival of whose actual arrival time is earlier than whose preferred arrival time.

Reference

Bailey, L., Mokhtarian, P.L. Little, A. (2008). The broader Connection Between Public Transportation, Energy Conservation And Greenhouse Gas Reduction, Report Prepared As Part Of TCRP Project J-11/Tasks Transit Cooperative Research Program, Transportation Research Board Submitted To American Public Transportation Association in http://www.apta.com/research/into/online/land_use.cfmi, accessed 17 April 2008.

The UK Standing Advisory Committee On Trunk Road Assessment (SACTRA) (1999). Transport And The Economy (Report To UK DETR). Retrieved From: http://webarchive.nationalarchives.gov.uk/ 20050301192906 ; http://dft.gov.uk/stellent/groups/dft-econappr/ documents/pdf/dft_econappr_pdf_022512.pdf

Wikipedia Contributors (2008). Arterial Roads In Wikipedia, The Free Encyclopeda, http://en.wikipedia.org/w/ index.php?title=Arterial_road&oldid=212832640(accessed May30,2008).

● Electronic vehicle invention casues passengers feel impact of undergrouund train transport to their working time efficiency

Any countries must need road, sea and air transport to assist businessmen to transport products in local or overseas. If the country's road , sea or air transport system service quality is poor. It will influence any products transport time, speed, inefficient transport to anywhere.

How to raise the country's transport system in order to improve efficiencies to let any businessmen can deliver their products to anywhere easily,e.g. warehouses, client homes, supermarkets destination in the most short time to avoid delay occurrence to let clients feel unsatisfactory or complaint their perform their delivery services poorly. I shall discuss the factors how to improve any countrues' transport systems to achieve the most efficient way as below:

Any countries' transport systems will create economic value, e.g. demonstrate value for money, economic worth, viable commercial worth, financial affordable worth, achieveable worth. Any countries' transport systems can bring welfare value by economics. It has direct relationship to take the form of measured economic activity, i.e. GDP. The form of measured economic activity can impact on any countries' economic economic geography, locally , regionally and nationally's local GDP impacts. The welfare impacts may include: leisure time savings, e.g. the local people drive cars or catch any public transportation tools to go to any geogrpahical location's shopping centers, big gardens, swimming pools, cinemas etc. places to carry on any kinds of leisure activities.

Environmental impacts may include avoiding noise, air pollution on road transportation aspect , when the main road is only on on focus on the main city,

but the city lacks other roads to let any drivers can choose them to drive, instead of the main road in the city. Then, when many cars are driven on the busy transport

time, e.g. morning working time or night busy time between 6:00 and 9:00 AM, between 6:00 and 9:00 PM. When either many working people need to catch public transport or drive themselves cars to go to offices to work or they need to catch pubic transport tools or drive themselves cars to home. Then, the only one main road problem will need them to stay themselves cars on roads, due to traffic jam or traffic accidence occurrence problem causes when many cars are driven on the road in the busy transport time. It will influence they can not go to offices or homes easily daily, even in the busy transport time, their cars' gas need to be used much to cause air pollution and traffic noise is easily caused easily in the busy transport time on the road. When the city has only one main road for drivers in the busy transport time. So, poor road transport system can bring poor impact on economic welfare benefits arising from proved labour supply from commuting, time savings, including exchequer benefits. Consequently, the county's GDP will be fallen down, due to labour market effects which do not add to welfare value.

Whether can poor transport system impact indirectly on GDP or not on local, regional , or national economic geography impacts? Does transport lead to greater economic activity i.e. higher GDP? DO they lead to change in economic activity location? Does transport impact the existence of business location and new economic activity opportunities? The measurement on every country's transport how impacts on economic change, facilitating geographic division of labour and specialization. It can be analyzed on these general aspects:

Costs and speed of travel time (Economic value of travel time savings) . Travel time savings to users from improved transport is a key of economic value, but it has only less influence,journey time reliability is more important to business frieght as well as business travellers, network connectivity enhancements as well as business travellers, network connectivity enhancement can help people and goods travel more quickly (i.e. linked to jounrey time and journey time reliability, as well as opening new destinations and new journeys, comfort and quality service provision is relevant to public transport, e.g. detering jounreys at particular times or by certain modes (e.g. overcrowding), impact on productivity at work for commuters, safety and security , due to loss of output from workers, transport accidents occur easily. All of these issues will impact any countries' standard of living to local people (geography) , even GDP income.

Why does the direct and indirect effects of transportation have a positive impact on the economic growth and development of a country? Does it influence acccess to goods, services and

employment opportunities in any regions? Underdeveloped countries must need to consider how transport system influences their economic growth. For example, the costs of transportation and production are reduced through timely delivery and enhancing the economies of scale in the production process, when the road is often traffic joam, gas cost, time waste , air pollution cost, noise has many roads, but if one lorry drivers needs drive more than one day to day to deliver goods to another city's warehouse every day. It will bring psychological pressure in terrible, when they need long time to drive on the road. They can not sleep easily because road accident will occur easily when they need to spend long time to drive lorries on the road.

So, how to solve the long driving time on road transport problem will be one issue concerns human life welfare benefit aspect, instead of economic benefit aspect. The transport system welfare worth needs to include human life worth. It is a valuable insight into the causality (ot lack of causality) between transport and economic growth and will serve to compare to any countries' national level and local geographical location level both.

In special, underdeveloped countries' public transport time whether it is long or short factor, it will influence workers their going to offices to work time. If they often need spend long time to catch buses, due to traffic jam,then it will influence their efficiences to be reduced, productive number is influenced to reduce also, because traffic jam causes they often go to offices too lately.It can influence workers' bad emotion to work every day. So, traffic jam will bring negative relationship between low efficiency and bad emotion to the workers, because they need to spend long time to wait, public transportation tools and traffic jam also influence their working emotion. Consequently, service and working performance will be influenced to poor, because long time traffic jam problem causes their bad emotion to work. It is one critical factor in the path of more widely spread economic growth and urbanization for traffic jam problem to underdeveloped countries.

However, transport system can also influence developed countries' economy. How does it influence on environmental impacts aspect from mature stage. Its business activities must raise, dramastic expansion during this period, such as underdeveloped country, US, UK. In order to acheive long term sustainable development , new demands are being placed on transport sector, such as underground mass transit rail transport , ferry, local air frieght transport, train , e.g. Japan, Fance, US high speed prior rail. Because their developed countries , business and entertainment activities needs increase, it influences high time efficient and rapid speed public transportation tools needs are also needed in societies. These new technological public transport tools invention will impact on climate, noise, human health, land use and damage to ozene layer, acidification aspects, instead of economic beneficial aspect.

For long -term sustainable development to be achieved, the various activities within developed and underdeveloped societies must be adapted to what can be tolerated by humans and by the natural environment. Transport is an activity which affects humans and the natural environment for both the development of society as a whole as well as for the mobility for the individual. For Swedish underdeveloped country example, air pollution in Swedish urban areas has beed reduced, but in many places concentrations of certain substances deiving from transport activities are still at unacceptable levels and much more has to be done. Carbon dioxide emissions and noise are examples of environmental problems demanding further efforts. Measures to limit the exploitation of valuable natural and cultural environments to protect biological diviersity are also needed. So, if Swedish still hopes to develop its tourism industry to attract many travellers to choose to travel itself country. It needs to solve environmental problems from different modes of transport are of different dimensions, such as improving its air transport to avoid cause different problems and rail transport differs in turn from road transport.

The transport problem to Swedish may include poor technological communication information to its public and purchasers of transportation and communication services as to the environmental effects of different solutions is significant in creating the demand for environmentally sound public transport service concepts. It is therefore important that such lacking high technological communication and information system is presented in as completem accurate and clear way as a method for non-monetary comparison of the environmental public transport service system aspect.

In real, it's public tranport service system is needed to be improved and upgraded in order to let travellers feel Swedish's any rail, underground train, ferry, bus , taxi etc. different public transport travelling service can provide excellent performance to serve their travelling passengers, when they need to catch any kinds of public transport tools to go to travel. They can feel convenient and comfortable to attract them to visit Swedish to travel again. Then, its tourism industry GDP income will be raised, if Swedish government can innovate any new kinds of purchase ticket equipment to install in and public transport stations to let travelling passengers feel that they do not need to spend long time to queue to buy tickets to catch ferry, train, underground mass transit rail on stations conveniently. Because long time purchase ticket queue waiting will cause travellers feel its public service performance dissatisfaction and they will complain , even they won't choose to catch the kind of public transport, even the travellers won't choose to travel Swedish again, if they feel Swedish is one developed country, but it neglects to take care about travellers' catching public transport travelling service needs.

It is one poor or bad feeing to let travellers choose to Swedish again. Hence, Swedish needs to improve its public transport service performance in order to achieve to raise their comfortable and satisfactory catching public transport tools needs to let travellers to feel. They may include efficient land use for transportation tools, comprising issues concerning natural and cultural environment, natural resources, biological diversity and aesthetics, noise reducing, public transportation energy consumption and time consumption reducing, raising public transport service facilities performance functions and other issues concerning the model. For example, Swedish government can facilitate the public transport price conparison and journey time spending comparison information gathering enquiring machines public transportation selection method of public transportation services to let every travellers can evaluate different modes of public transport when they are staying in ferry, bus, train, underground mass transit rail, taxi stations.

A travelling family can seek its sustainable transport selection system for passenger transport tool. When they touch the enquiry machine, they can compare busm ferry, train, underground train, taxi price and journey spending time from their transportation stations to another destinations. Then, travelling passengers can compare these public transport tools ticket prices, journey spending time immediately when they touch the public transport enquiring machines in stations any time. Then, they can make the most righ choice to decide whether they ought catch which kind of public transport tool to arrive the another journey destination. It is one every attractive high technological enquiry method to help any travelling passegners to choose which kind of public transport tool, it can be the most cheap transport tool at the moment in any public transport stations. So , for developed countries innovative its public transport service performance will need future passengers' journey needs daily. Hence, they can not neglect how to improve public transport service needs to satisfy passengers to feel satisfaction, if Sweden government hopes its tourism industry can raise GDP income in long time.

CHAPTER TWO

Can COVID 19 disease influence business development

COVID -19 disease how influence businesses may experience either growing life cycle stage or decline life cycle stage.

Nowadays, we are facing global economic recession period, since COVID 19 human mouth disease effect can bring economic crisis. Can it influence businesses feel difficult to adapt how global economic recession change after their decline life cycle stage? However, the effects of COVID 19 spreading will have wider implication , not just on how economies function, but also on how consumers behave, across china, Asia-pacific and around the world. Another effect of China;s economic rise is its influence in the adoption and adaption to new technological invention to manufacture , e.g. manufacturing robotic products had sold to China factories to replace workers to manufacturer products. It also will influence many China manufacturing workers lose jobs, when many China factories apply manufacture robotics to replace them in nowadays economic recession period.

Considering the adoption of online-offline shopping and home online office tasks, they are influenced by COVID-19 human disease influence, it also influences on regional travel in China, even global travel income is also reducing, because many travelers feel afraid to catch air planes to avoid to get COVID 19 human disease when they are sitting in close window airplanes by air . HOwever, COVID 19 also influences global consumer behavior changes to online shopping, because many people are afraid to enter crowd shops to avoid get COVID 19 human disease easily. So global shops will lose many visiting shop consumers, if they do not decide to attempt to open online stores to let customers to apply internet to buy their products. So, COVID 19 human mouth disease induced changes in consumer behavior. Shop online will be one new trend to influence young and old consumers make shopping from online stores. They will enquire whether the kind of product is worth to choose to buy by social media, e.g. facebook, online post . Hence, COVID19 human mouth disease may influence global economic recession, but it also brings e-commerce boom chance, when many consumers are fear to enter any crowd shops , when they need to stay long time in any shops. Then, they get COVID 19 human mouth disease chance will increase. Hence, it will influence many customers reduce to visit shops times, but it also creates online-shopping new business model . For example, China families are renewing their joy in home cooking. Onlins cooking videos are helping with the discovery od new recipes, new ways to create dishes , and new influences. So, opportunities are opening for more cleaning products, new ways to clean and new home hacks from online videos will bring global home consumers spend more time on their wellness or beauty routines ? So, COVID-19 disease also influences many families choose to cook dinner at homes at nght. Restaurants will lose many eating clients, because they are fear to enter restaurants to eat together to avoid to get COVID19 human mouth disease. But, it also creates home cooking products sale chance, e.g. rice cookers, dishes or any cooking tools because many families choose to cool at home. Hence, in some situation, economic recession will create new business chance , such as online store or rice cooker sale increases, they may be influenced in this COVID 19 human mouth disease occurrence environment.

Economic recession also influences business strategy changes. Many companies seem to be applying many aspects of a retrenchment approach , e.g. reduced fixed costs, narrower product offering, reduced staffs, but also there are some aspects of an investment approach which can be observed , because customers number will be influenced to reduce in economic recession environment. Companies have felt the robustness and quality of the approaches being applied had been allowed to decline. As a consequence of the challenges of a recession, urgent improvement have needed to be made because factories will reduce workers number to avoid salary expenditure spending more , but customers umber reduced in recession environment .

Hence, they will choose to buy manufacturing robotics to replace workers. If robotics can be improved to be proficient manufacture. Then, they won't need to buy many robotics to help them to replace to replace many workers to manufacture any products efficiently. So, manufacturing and improvement to robotics number demand may increase to any factories , e.g. vehicle manufacture, electronic products, e.g. computer hime cooking electronic products , e.g. rice cookers, heaters etc. products may be manufactured by manufacturing robotics. It creates the manufacturing robotic sale improvement quality chance in recession environment. It may impact on medium, or long term, it depends on how long time of recession. So, economic recession may bring robotic manufacture industry boom , when electronic products manufacturers need many improved robotics to replace workers in factries in order to reduce spending too much salaries expenditure in recession.

It is one external environmental factor to influence sudden manufacture robotic industry boom absolutely ,because electronic manufacturer's manufacturing robotic needs increases in recession environment. So, robotic manufacturers' strategy need to change , such as how to improve any manufacturers' needs in recession, e.g. manufacturing robotic product categories, market segments, geographic areas, core technologies, reliability , price, customisation, robotic manufacturing efficiency how to be improved of business.Change strategy to any manufacturing robotics manufacturers. So, recession may influence some kinds of manufacturing robotics' needs raise in robotic manufacturing market.

● How recession influences the role of advertising changes?

Advertising plays a key role in a dynamic economy. It may provide valuable information about products and services in an efficient manner, communicates client value, builds brand awareness and creates demand. However, when one country is experiencing recession, how it influences the country's businessmen spending on advertisement behaviors? Due to clients number reduces, a company usualy cuts come from the advertising budget than companies begin to cut back on advertiseing during an economic recession, they become less visible to the public because they predict clients number ought reduce next three months, even half year or one year. It depends on how long economt recession occurs. So, economic recession many impact any companies' advertising budget expenditure to be reduce . How much on the reduction on advertising budget expenditure, it depends on the company predicts how many clients number will reduce.However, due to advertising number reduces, it can influence consumer behavior changes indirectly.

In economic boom environment, consumers can watch to different kinds advertisement from television. Advertisement may bring positive alternative evaluation phase of biying decision-making process is bring exposed to buy several communication messages. In such an economic boom environment, any organizations may be clearly heard by the consumers, after any advertisement programs are broadcasted on television. Therefore, advertisemtn can persuade clients to choose to buy the kind of product after the kind of product advertisement is broadcasted from television absolutely.

However, when recession occurs, any companies; advertisement time is shortened , even number is reduced . Hence, they can not receive any client's positive or negative feedback immediately in short time afer advertisements are broadcasted from television . So, recession may influence advertisement time is shortened and number is rediced . On consequence, companies can not have any repsonse to know whether how market or customers' demand is changing to themselves products in shor time.

However, recession may bring worse advertisement effect to influence any businesses . On one hand, there is a negative economic recession environment because of the negative media reporting, these would be a decline in demand for the products and services and eventually companies would want to save more than they spend , But in the other hand, when the companies cut back advertiseing expenditures, they become less visible to public. Hence recession may influence many companies brand image will be lost, due to spending on advertisement expenditure wil reduce. Then, clients number may be influenced to reduce, because they can not watch the kind of product advertisment from television home often.

When one country is encountering recession, how are the various components of household consumption affected ? How is the impact of the recesion distributed across socio-demographic group? How does the recession compare to previous recessions? When book will boom? In fact, any country's recession may impact consumer behavior changes, it depends on these factors: age, race, education and wealth groups resulted in a decline in consumption inequality. The rich group is the " wealth effect influence group" when recession comes, it may influence their wealth reduces, so their enjoyment dsires will be influenced to reduce, e.g. purchase expensive cars driving enjoyment desires, purchase expensive house living enjoyment desires. If one rich person loses jobs , it may influence him to spend less time to drive themselves cars, so consumption of gasline will be influenced to reduce.

Economic theory (e.g. consumer behavioral economic theory) predicts that when economic recession occurs, it will cause many businesses may experience decline cycle life stage rapidly, that link between income shocks and consumption has close relationship, such as rich person consumer group, if his income reduces, then he will buy less gas to drive himself car, even if he loses his job in recession environment, he will choose to sell his car to exchange cash. Hence, consumption may fall as a direct consequence of a fall in income induced by job loss, reduced hours or productivity and negative returns from assets, if there are long term changes to a household's econmic resource in recession environment. Hence, in recession environment, job loss or income reduction factors that may affect consumers and their shopping attitudes in the recession period. Otherwise, for low income group, recession may influence food consumption to low income consumer behavior changes to worse. Because low income person may reduce income ot lose job, then cheap food consumption will be influenced to worse to low income consumer group.

In recession period, if the food price is raised , due to the cost increase of food, it will lead to change in the reductin on quantity and type of food being purchase to low income food buyers. This may lead to a reduction in the quantity of food consumed and/or the substitution of high-priced food for cheaper food, which is often less nutritous and of worse quality. Hence in recession perios, low income food consumers will consider whether the kind of food price has how much increase or decrease. They won't consider the quantity of food consumed for maintaining energy balance and the quality of food consumed for maintaining ample intakes of protains, fats and micronutrients, such as vitamins, minerals and trace elements on food issue. So, if the kind of food price reduced in recession period, it ought may attract many low income food consumers number, even its food nutritious is worse. Hence, if the kind of meat price can be reduced in recession , the cheap types of meat consumption to low income consumer may be increased, even its nutritious is worse to compare the recession occurs before period.

On conclusion, in either economic recession or boom period, in general, consumer behavior will be influenced to change. Some products may be influenced to have higher sale in recession period, e.g. home electronic rice cookers , due to COVID 19 human mouth disease influenced many households choose to cook dinner at home at ight. Otherwise, some products may be influenced to have lowr sale., e.g. expensive cars sale in recession period, many high income people may lose jobs or reduce salaries , then it will influence their car purchase desires to be reduced. But if COVID 19 human mouth disease has medicine to kill this kind of disease. Then, economy will boom, many households will choose to go to restaurants to eat dinner. The, the electronic rice cookers sale number may reduce, when they reduce time to cook at home at night. Hence, it explains why economic recession or boom period may have impact to influence consumer behavior in behavioral economic view.

Applying business development strategy to raise the educational robotic manufacturer sale number in recession period

● What does business development strategy ?

An effecting business development strategy ought have these five steps: The first step is market analysis. Who are your clients , knowledge of your market? Second step is how to adopt for each penetration, your business needs to learn how to adopt for each group of clients, your first need to review your own capacbility. It is important that you are realistic and honest with yourselves over where clients truly sit, learn how to classify your clients into similar groups relative is the scale of the opportunity. Third step learns how to review your performance , market matrix to plot your results to help you determine your market penerstion. In addition, it will help you then discuss and consider various strategies for growth. By potting your clients you will get a sense of where your strengths and weaknesses are against the opportunity that total market offer.Fourth step learns how to consider alternative growth strategies on the market matrix. The final step , you need to consider these questions in order to decide whic is the most effective strategy for your business. For example, which model is the most (least effective? Why? which model work best for line managers, HR are finance, why? How might we most effectively progress from one model to the most reasonable questions?) Then, you will need to decide how to launch new services, new products, opening new markets, how accessing new geographic territories.

● How to apply business development strategy to help educational robotic manufacturers to enter traditional education market ?

Many thinkers concern robots that are used in manufacturing workplaces, homes, roads, hospitals and care centre aspect, but they don't feel robotics may be possible to apply on social service aspect, e.g. educational service aspect . In fact, robotic may have both functions. Industrial robotics, e.g. manufacturing function as well as service robotics, e.g. professional robotcs, medical robotics, entertainment robotics, e.g. toy and education robotics and service robotics , e.g. personal and domestic robotics.

Educational robotic is on the birth stage in its industry life cycle. So, any educational robotic products will need time to persuade schools or any educational institutions to buy their products to assist teachers to teach students in classrooms. The question is how to apply business development strategy to help the educational robotic manufacturer to develop its educational robotic products to persuade educational clients to choose to buy ? I shall attempt to explain as below:

Due to educational robotic product is one new educational tool to assist any schools to buy to assist teachers to improve teaching service performance to let students to feel more learning satisfaction, so any educational robotic products must need time to introduce whether what it can bring schools benefits to let students and teachers to feel. When robotic can be popular to use on manufacturing, educational service industries aspect, e.g. warehouse , factory, shopping center, even restaurant's kitchen cooking robotics, office environment's accounting, law draft etc. clerical robotics may be invented to replace human 's general simple tasks. However, if future robots can be applied to educational aspect, e.g. classroom, school teaching students. Can educational robotic may assist or replace teachers to teach students in clasrooms? Will future teachers be replaced by teaching robotics . I shall attempt to explain whether it is possible that educational robotic can be developed to global educational organizations successfully as below:

Robotic technology has been invented to own " mind " ability, e.g. writing words, writing song, simple calculation tasks reading tasks . So, future robotics can be invented to own " mind " ability, when robotics' mind ability can be improved to own how to " communication" ability and " analytical" ability. Then can it be possible to apply robotics to do teaching tasks in classrooms, e.g. learning any books , the it applies the book's contents to analyze any "knowledge" in order to follow the logic mind to teach students in classroom. It is one major factor to influence any schools to explain why they need to buy any educational robotic in schools in any educational robotic product business development strategy. So, they need to find whether what their educational robotic strengths , any competitors won't own or their product weaknesses, they need to improve their educational robotic products in order to attract educational organizations to choose to buy.

Can future teaching robotics learn to do teacher individual same education tasks? It will be absolute competitive point to any educational robotic product manufactures. If it is true, can teaching robotics may be trained to exceed teacher individual teaching skill? It is another competitive point to any educational robotic product manfacturers. Is it ethic to apply robotic to teach students to replace teachers if teaching robotic can perform better teaching service to compare teachers? If the eduational robotic manufactuer can persude the school can accept eduational robotic ethic issue to assist or replace teachers to do teaching tasks, then it's sale chance will raise. So, ethic to educational robotic will be another factor to develop the educational robotic business. Can teachers be teaching robotic's teaching assistant role if teaching robotics can have teaching ability to teacher in the school? So, if the educational robotic manufacturer can persuade the school to feel that its products can be teacher's assistant to improve their performance to let students learn more easily. The educational robotics manufacturer may develop its product to sell in this educational market more easily, in business development strategy view.

All of these will be future any one educational robotic development challenges if they hope their products can sell more easily. They also need to know to let schools to know these disadvatages to their products to become advatanges in order to attract they to choose to buy their producte more easily. Such as what potential harmful consequences may come from the inventing of teaching robotics? What happends to important education moral, such as teacher or school privacy then robotic are starting to become an teaching tool to the school? Do such robotics hace any roght and responsibilities if the class has many students learning ability are influenced to poor or examination results are poor when the educational robotic has been bought to assist the school teachers to teach their students? Why does the school need to buy educational robotic to do teaching tasks? Any school organizations must need any one educational robotic product seller to answer any one of above questions, before they decide to buy their products. So, they must need to ensure teaching robotics will be used to help the school to teach students to learn more understanding to compare teachers only.

● Future educational robotic are applied on development teaching maths market

In the future, business development to educational robotic market may be teaching maths. I shall explain as below:

It is possible that students can use mobile robotic to learn mathematics subject to compare teachers more easily. Why? For example, young age from 4 to 14 age, they may apply mobile robotics to learn add, multiple, divided, simple math equation more understanding than math teaches. Robotic kints and apps is currently available on the maket for teacher of 4 to 14 age students,due to mobile , kits app price is cheap. So, they can be popular to be accepted by any primary schools , even in secondary schools, robotics may be applied to teach computer science, statistical methods subjects of one robotic kit for teach team of 2 to 3 students, short theory lessons , and tutorials to link theory and practice, realistic but affordable tasks linked with curricular subjects, teachers at ease with the robotic etc. So, future primary and secondary , even university teachers may need to choose the more suitable robot kit for their students,and carefully design where and how to use it and with which role.In fact, children will be possible to raise interest to learn when they can contact for any kind of teaching robotic to learn maths in classrooms together. So, teaching robotics may help 4 to 14 children students to raise learning interest instead of learning about ability.

In the future, robotic role is school may be one tool to engage the students as teachers role may be transfer base knowledge when teachers teach maths, geography, statistics, computer science subjects to promary , secondary even university students. This is one good example , whether what subjects robotic may be applied when it is invented to own human mind and anlaytical skill and communication ability. Robotics can perform more better to be applied to teach these subjects. It can let students to understand easily, e.g. understanding how to create equations that describe numbers a relationship understanding solving equations as a process of reasoning and explain the equations and inequalities in one variable, helping students to find different solutions, then best solves the problem , given the criteria and the constraints, helping students have more understanding how science knowledge is based upon logical and conceptual connections between evidence and explanations, even robotc can ask questions that can be investigated within the scope of the classroom, outdoor environment, and museums and other public faciltities with available resources and when appropriate frame a hypothesis based on observation and scientific principles. Even, robotics may help students to learn how construct, use and present oral and written arguments supported by evidence and scientific reasoning to support or refute an explanation or a model for a phenomenon, or robot can hep students to learn how obtain, evaluate and communicate information in 6-8 builds on k-5 and progresses to evaluating the merit and validity of ideas and methods, integiate qualitative scientific and technical information in written text with that contained in media and visual displays to clarify cliams and findings, helping students to anlyze data from texts to determine similarities and differences among several design solutions to identify the best characteristics of each that can be combined into a new solution to better meet the criteria for success, even helping students to learn how analyze data in 9-12 builds on k-8 and progresses to introducing more detailed statistical anslysis, the comparision of data sets for consistency and the use of models to generate and analyze data, analyze data using tools, technologies , and/or models e.g. computational, mathematical in order to make valid and variable scientific claims or determine and optinal design solution more easily than human teacher. So, there are human-made educaton machine advantage to students more than human teacher.

Educational robotic has been introduced as a powerful, in fact, flexible teaching / learning tool stimulating learns to control the behavior of tangible model using specific programming languages (graphical, or textual and involving them actively in authentic problem -solving activities. Howeverm in future educational robotic development, it may be divided two separate categories as below:

Robotics as learning object: This first category includes educational activities where robotics is being studied as a subject on its own. It includes educational activities aimed at configuring a learning environment that will actively involve learners in the solution of authentic problems, facing on robotics -related subjects, such as robot construction, robot programming and artificial intelligence as well as robotic as learning tool: In the frame of this second category, robotics is proposed as a tool for teaching and learning other school subjects at different school levels. Robotics as learning tool is usually, seen as an interdisciplinary, project -based learning activity drawing mostly on science, maths, informatics and technology and offering major new benefits to education in genera at all levels. However, I believe the role of teacher is crucial for the successful industry of technological and innovations in classrooms, when robotics are been particiapted to any education tasks in classrooms. Schools can focuse on the training of prospective and in-service teachers in the use of robotics technologies through courses.

In future electronic learning environment, robotics can be participated, such as recognised their active participation in all sessions of the course and their creative involvement even in the theoretical parts introducing principles and methodology for designing robotic-enhanced projects, very much liked the activity-orientation of the educational content, acknowledged the central role of the e-workspace during the face-to-face meetings and beyond ehem in enhancing sense of community, acknowledged the potential of educational robotics as a teaching tool but also as a subject, in different disiplines , such as technology, informatics and engineerinfg, highly appreciated the opportunity to create their projects.

How to develop robotic in technological subjects on teaching, learning and educational aspect? Learners can be encouaged hen robotics participate actively in the learning process. Through robotic learners build something on their own, preferably a tangible object, that they can both touch and find meaningful. In robotic learners are invited to work experiments or problem-solving with selective use of available resources, according to their own interest, search and learning strategies. Robotics can help them to seek solutions to real world problems, based on a technological framework meant to engage students' movitation. So, when students can have control of specific robotc in a rich learning environment, the construction of robots and programs to control them the emphasis might move on interesting learning actiities in the frame of specific learning areas , such as science and technology. Thus, the design of robotic construction activities is associated with the fulfillment of a project aimed at solving a problem. In such a learning environment, learning is driven by the problem to be solved. To engage students in activities requiring to design and manufacture real objects, i.e. robotic structures that make sense for themselves and should devise activities that will encourage students to support in order experiment. So, robotic participation any science experiments, they may encourage students to create problem solving and combining interdisiplinary concepts from different knowledge areas,: science, mathematics , technology and research educational tasks, the role of students will change, when preparing a work with a programmable robotics studies experiment with simple programmable sobotics devices , e.g. a car-robot, motors, sensor etc. Students are asked to synthesize their finds and reach conclusions and solutions to the problem uner investigation. SO, robotic is educaional participation to any scientfic technological or research experiments, they may help students to work with creativity , imagination and independence and finally organize the evaluation of the activity in collaboration ith studens. Also robotic participation to any technological or scientific research experiemtn, it also change teacher role . The teacher is such a constructist theoretical framework, like that teacher 's role that does not transfer ready knowledge to students, but rather acts as a organizer, coordinator and facilitator of learning for students. when educational robotics participate to any science or technological any research experiments, students may be organize the learning environment, raise the question , problem to be solved by students allow students to work with creativity, imagination and independence and finally organize the evaluation of the activity in collaboration with students. So, any educational robotic manufacturers must let their school clients to feel all these benefits which can bring to let students to raise learning abilty and learning interest to compare that are only taught by teachers, if they hope their educational robotics can be sold successfully in business development strategy view.

Learning behavioral economy to solve social challenges

● Why do some social challenges may influence customers number ?

In our societies , we shall have different challenges to our every day. However, in general , the challanges seem that they do not have relate to influence businessmen profit, but in fact, these social challenges have relationship to influence business profit and clients number. I shall indicate some social challenges to explain why these social challenges may influence any business profit indirectly as below:

In investment or raving individual preference decision aspect, for some people , it may be interesting or fun to think cbout the best investments or the right health care plan. But, for other people, these choices are unpleasant, they may be persuaded to buy anythings, e.g. car, computer. So, if car seller can have persuasive methods to influence many people feel the health care plan or investment plan is not prefereable choices, driving car enjoyable feeling or material enjoyment is the most preference choice. Then I believe that the car seller's car selling number may increase, because some people greatly enjoy thinking about their pension and the best investment or health care insurance preferable decision, their decision had been influenced to choose to buy the car seller's cars. When they feel driving car enjoyable feeling is more important than future benefit.

Hence, in behavioral economy view, they had felt the driving car benefit is much to compare pension investment or health care insurance future benefit. The question is how to car seller can persuade these investment ot pension plan or health care preference decision individual to change purchase car driving decision>

I suggest that the car seller may have discount or cash coupon or installment payment method to attract them to consider , instead of advertisement promotion method. because this preference investment or pension saving or health care plan decision individual customer group will be more difficult to persuade them to choose to buy car immediately at this moment. Hence, if the car seller can not implement cheap car discount strategy, it will be difficult to attract this prefeence long term future benefit consumer to make purchase ca r decision easily. Because they think pension or investment or health care plan ce help them to bring long term future benefit, also it means that purchase car may only bring short term present benefit. It is general social behavioral consumption model to influence their purchase choice. Hence, I assume that general social long term future benefit product or service, e.g. insurance, investment , pension may influence th scocial shor tterm present benefit product , e.g. car consumer. It is the main reason, it can explain why car sellers can not persuade this long term future benefit consumers to make decision to buy their cars easily, when they have no enough money to spend to buy car and make investment, saving , medical care insurance , pension plan in the same time. They must need to make either purchase car or insurance etc. decision in our nowadays societies.

So, in behavioral economic view, it explains why consumer individual purchase choice behavior has relationship to himself/herself spending budget. I assume that it has two kinds of behavioral economic consumers. One kind if long term future economic benefit in preference more than short term present economic benefit, such as purchase car and investment or health care plan insurace saving term present benefit consumer, he / she considers to earn driving enjoyment at this moment is not preference than purchase insurance or investment future benefit decision . So, our society, any business will encounter these two kinds of behavioral consumer. They persuade either long term futuer benefit consumecrs or short term present benefit consumer to change himself/herself products or services more easily. Otherwise, such as if car seller can not implement coupon or cash reward or discount or installment cash payment strategy to attracr the long term future benefit consumer. Then, it will lose this group car customers number absolutely. So, it explains why businessmen need to learn consumer behavioral consumption model in order to increase client number more easily.

" Social welfare" usually measured by people's prefences, and it also focuses for the conventional economists, on how to maximize social welfare. What then is the task of behavior law and economics? Such as, this cate seller case example, whether what social welfare the car seller can bring to society when the individual decides to buy its car to drive or when the individual chooses to buy health care insurance or pension plan or investment . When he/she chooses to buy health care insurance or make pension plan or buys any companies' shares. Then, these investment service companies will bring what benefits to our society? So, instead of consumer benefit, we also need to consider whether the kind of product or service will bring what long term social benefit . However, I think that when global many people own cars, then many cars are driven on the roads, it will bring serious air pollution to influence our health. Then, when many people are got lung diseases by air pollution. Then, many people will need to pay more medical expense. It will be long term negative medical cost increasing expense to future us, but it also bring possible income for insurance firms, when many people plan to buy medical care plans when they feel air pollution will influence them to need to pay future medical expense. So, it seems that the effect on many people own cars and their driving behaviors will bring serious air pollution, but it will also create the health care medical insurance need to be increased due to many people feel air polluton will bring lung disease and they need to pay long time medical expensein the future long time in possible. So, many people driving behavior may bring air pollution, but it also bring medical insurance need increases in our society in possible. It means that air pollution may create medical insurance market develops in possible, such as most smokers say they would prefer not to smoke, and many pay money to join a program or obtain a drug that will help them quit.If many smokers forgive to smoke, then the medical care insurance need for smokers number may be influenced to reduce.

In social benefit view, medical insurance for smokers insurance will be influenced to reduce, due to many smokers forgive to smoke. Although, many smokers may get health, when they do not smoke, they do not pay to buy any cigeratte often, they can save more money, but cigeratte sellers and medical insurance service providers , their income must be influenced to reduce. Hence, when our society government's advertisement concerns smokers often smoke cigeratte, it may bring poor drug health or many cars air pollution, these two messages may influence or dissuade many smokers forgive to smoke or many people do not buy cars. They choose to catch public transportation, or owning car people who do not often drive cares, then car gas or fuel suppliers income will be influenced to reduce, due to many car owning people do not often drive cars or many people do not choose to buy cars. Then, car sellers' income wil be influenced to reduced. Moreover, in long term social influence, when many people do not feel lung disease . Then, the medical care insurance need will also influenced to reduce.

It may bring insurance industry develops in difficulty for lung dissease medical care insurance. So, it explains why consumer behavior may also influence our social economic development in long term . They have cause and effect close relationship. When many consumers individual forgive or dislike to do the behavior in habit, e.g. driving car behavior or smoking behavior. Then, it will influence car seller market and cigeratte seller market to be poor in any countries , even global market.

Hence, in our society, when one individual feels that he.she has individual challenge, it may be economic or emotion or health problem, such as smoking influences health case, driving influences air pollution case. These both kinds of individual behavior may influence the individual may need to spend money for lung disease if he/she has continue smoking habit every day or he/she often drives car . Then, the individual will seek methods to solve these possible occurrence of problems before they do not occur. As it occurs in the natural environment, e.g. air pollution or lung disease is caused by cars or smoking. When individual begins feel these negative effect may case, if he/she continues to do smoking or dirving car behavior. He/she will begins to find methods to solve problem, problem solving is defined as the self-directed cognitive -behavioral process by which an individual , couple or group, such as smokers and drivers group in our society, they attempt to identify or disciver effective solutions for specific problem encountered in everyday living. More specifically, this cognitive -behavioral process (a) makes available a variety of potentially effective solutions for a particular problem and (b) increases the probability of selecting the most effective solution from among the various alternatives (D'Zurilla & Gold field 1971).

reference

D' Zurilla, T. J. & Goldfield, M.R, (1991). Problem solving and behavior modification, Journal of abnormal psychology, 78, 107-126.

As this definition implies social problem solving is conceived as a conscious, rational, effortful, and purposeful activity. Depending on the problem solcing goals, this process may be aimed at changing the problematic situation for the better, reducing the emotional distress that it produces or both.

Hence, it implies that when any one feels he/she will have individual problem, e.g. health problem , economuc problem,emotion problem. He/she will avoid to continue to do the kind of behavior often every day ,e.g. smoking behavior or driving car behavior .When our society has many people make to forgive to do above themselves behaviors, such as smoking or driving habit. Then, it will influence cigeratte sale number and car sale numner to be reduced. So, when our society has any consumer groups, they forgive to do themselves behaviors in habit. Consequently, the kind of product seller or service provider may lose man customers. So, in our society , when one kind of product or service consumers , their habital behaviors are changed to reduce, then it may influence the kind of product sellers or service providers their income or clients number to be either decrease or increase. On conclusion, it explains that why social behavior has close relationship to influence business income or clients number in our societies.

Learning organizational life cycle stage strategies advantages

Any organizations may experience organizational life cycle stages from birth stage to growth stage to maturity , then it may also experience decline and/or regrow stages. But this two stages, they are not all organizations must may attempt to experience. It depends on whether economic environment how changes, organizational itself SWOT strengths and weaknesses etc. unpredicted factors to influence that when the organization will experience decline life cycle stage. It means that if the organization has very poor performance, then the organization has possible to experience decline life cycle stage in short time or long time. Otherwise, if the organizationhas very good performance, it ought not experience decline life cycle stage in short time, when it can reach mature stage in its the topest level. Even, when the organization has poor performance, so it is experiencing decline stage, but if it may implement effective strategies to help itself organization to develop . Then, if its strategies are very effective , in consequence, the organization ought may experience regrowing stage to re-experience its mature life cycle stage again. So, it seems that if the organization can have very good performance. Client number can increase significant as well as profit can also growth rapidly. Then, the organization ought may experience long time in mature life cycle stage or it means that it will be difficult to reach decline life cycle stage. Unless, some sudden inpredicted economic environment, or strong competitors etc. influence its performance, then they will have chance to cause it experiences to decline life cycle stage from mature stage suddenly. Hence, all organizations must need to experience birht life cycle stage in beginning to this stage.

However, when the business founder starts to set up his/her business. He/she needs time to deal any difficulties,e.g. how to advertise his/her products to let customers have much knowledge, promote them to sell to market, how to implement strategies to solve organizational challenges. So, in birth stage, any organizations ought feel difficult to improve its whole performance or evaluate whether its future performance can improve to be better or can not improve or worse. Then, when the organization operates one period, it ought experience to growth stage, but it still depends on external factors to influence whether when it may experience growth stage, the factors may include: Whether strategies can be effective, economic environment is good or bad, customers purchase desire level is high or loe, cost expenditure is high or low etc. difficult factor.

So, before any organizatons may experience growth stage, there are many different complex factors to influence whether they can succeed to experience this stage easily. If the organization can not implement any effective strategies to solve its customers purchase emotion challenges, then its business is difficult to continue grow, also it means that the organization can not growor expand its business easily. Due to it can not continue to develop its business easily. It must not reach mature life cycle stage easily. Thus, any organizations can reach mature life cycle stage. It represents that its business has good strategies to solve any challenges in order to its products can attract customers to choose to buy or it can provide good service performance to satisfy clients needs to compare irs competitors in this market successfully.

In fact, it is not all organizations can attempt to experience the mature life cycle stage. This stage is any organization individual the topest stage. In this stage, the organization may have many clients increasing number significantly every year, its market can continue expand, profit can continue increases . All is the best to any organizations, if it can reaches this stage . All many organizations may only experience birth stage or growing stage . They reach this either birth or growth stage, then they have none good strategies to compete their clients number can not increase, but only decreases, profit reduces , even loss. They can not know how to change strategied to improve their performance or competitive effort to fight this competitors. Then, their businesses can not continue grow or expand. So, they have more chance to experience decline stage after either birth or growth stage only. They can not reach mature life cycle stage to attempt the topest level in whole business (organizational) life cycle stage or process. Thus, it brings these questions: Why do organizations need to learn organizational life cycle stages? What advantages to bring if they can attempt to learn how to reach growth or mature life cycle stages easily? I shall explain as below:

● Why do organizations need to spend time to learn how may experience different business life cycle stages?

The business life cycle is the progression of a business in phases over time and is most commonly divided into five stages: Launch or birth, growth, maturity and decline or regrow. Each company begins its operations as a business and usually by launching new products or services. Because any organizations will encounter challenges in every stages . If they know what factos may help them to enter another new stage of business life cycle or what challenges may threaten them can not enter another new business life cycle stage easily. Because businessman need to learn and how adjust their business model to ensure profitability. That is why an awareness of what stage of the business life cycle , you are currently it can be helpful. Hence, how to maximize each stage of the business life cycle, the businessmen might still need to learn how to work in order to improve performance when the businessmen are experiencing any one life cycle stage. Moreover, each business life cycle stage comes still need to learn how to turn a profit and the first outlines of their governance and compliance and this is one big reason why most businesses fail at this stage.

So, I assume that business life cycle stage is similar to school examination, the student needs to spend time to learn in the birth learning stage, then he needs to test in the growth learning stage, next is examination in the mature learning stage, if the student fails, t is decline learning stage to the school. It may be due to the teachers can not teach students to learn easily. So, these are many students fail in tests or examinations. So, if the school teachers can improve teaching methods to let many students may earn high grades in tests or examinations. Then, the school may experience growth, even mature teaching life cycle stage in short time rapidly . Hence, teaching quality can improve or not , it will influence any school organizations ought feel to schools to learn how to improve teaching methods or strategies in order to let students can experience the maturity learning stage or it can also experience the maturity teaching stage. It means that it ought learn how to improve its teachers teaching service performance to satisfy students learning needs if it hopes to reach maturity learning and teaching life cycle stage in short time for itself school organization benefit.For example, the organization founder may ask himself/herself why he/she wants to start this business, learns how to manage exployees strategies? It is the learning needs in the third stage, such as maturity stage. Otherwise, in the first stage of the business entity birth life cycle is sometimes called the seed stage and a matter of iteraing, testing an learning , and trying again, knowing that the businessman is unlikely to have.

What advantages may bring to the organization if it can attempt to learn how to solve different challenges in different business life cycle stages ? What advantages to the organization, if it can know how to experience every business life cycle stage?

In fact, the business life cycle is the progression of a business in phases over time, and is consumer segments by advertising their comparative advantages and vale. For example, when the business is experiencing growth stage , in the growth phase, the business founder needs to spend time to learn how his company can experience rapid sales growth. This learning may assist his business to develop his business to enter next mature how stage easily , for example, he can learn how the rapid growth stage takes advantage from the proven sales model, e.g. online sale or traditional visiting shop sale model which is more suitable to his business, marketing model and operations model, e.g. how to advertise his product or promote his products can affect more audiences concern this will see the businessmen's jounrey from idea to start up, and if successful, how to keep to stay long time in the mature stage. Rememeber, when having a successful business model behind any businessmen is undoubtedly an advantage, it is not a disadvantage when the founder spends more time to learn hoe to run his business. In fact, he won't waste his time to learn how to improve his business in different business life cycle stages. So, a tactical plan will take any business strengths and reduces to avoid weakness cause to influence its development. So, knowing where you small product is in its product life cycle, it is important to continue to develop your business successfully. SO, any impacts of all life cycle stages, any businesses need to be considered comprehensively , for one new technological product firm example, its new technological product life cycle begins with the introduction or birth stage. The high technological product company must succeed at both developing new product and managing them in the face of changing tastes, competitors' technologies similar change. So, it is what it needs to learn in this stage for this new product technological firm preparing development to next growth stage.

On the conclusion, learning how to achieve in every business life cycle stage, it can bring these benefits to any organizations, such as : they can understand and redefine this role from a more, if the organization ony to learn sale frameworks what it could have picked up. It is not enough, because most organizations will only find that a majority of their total sale number which is to use solely supplier-specific data about the life cycle, but they neglect how to set targets to learn how to improve their sale to be better in the future time, it is one important factor explain why many organizations only reach the growth stage, but they can not experience to next mature stage more easily, due to they do not consider how to implement strategies in order to achieve their next targets. They feel often implment targets which will help them to know whether they need to how to do in order to improve their businesses to satisfy clients needs. As with any effort in your organization, communication plays a critical role, craft machine learning to predict and manage human for remote teams to work through the innovation lifecycle, serve them well. Any organizations need to learn how to satisfy any customer individual purchase jounrey (called purchase experience) which the customer has with the organization, because when the organization can learn how to satisfy any client individual real need in any life cycle stage. On consequence, its clients number with have possible to influence increase. Thus, any organizations can bot neglect to learn how to satisfy client individual real purchase experience need in any life cycle stages because improvement to salepeople sale performance, they need spend time to learn in every time sale experience . When the organization can build excellent sale teams, then they may help it to build famous loyalty and good client relationship in order to expand its business more easily. Hence, in any businesses' life cycle stages, they must need to spend time to learn how to improve product quality service performance to bring customers' satisfactory emotion in order to expand their business developmenr more easily. So, i recommend that all small organizations expand to large size, they must need time to learn and attempt to find the best methods to solve any difficulties when they are facing in any one business cycle stage, if they want to expand their businesses successfully.

● The relationship between learning change management and rapid reaching mature life cycle

It is one good question: Can the manager or CEO help whole organization to develop rapidly if he/she attempt to learn how to help his/her organization to implement different strategies to solve different challenges in different business life cycle stages? Does it easy to help the organization to grow up when a learning CEO or learning manager accepts to learn anything to compare a non learning manager in different business life cycle stages? Has it relationship between learning or non learning manager and rapid experiencing business life cycle stage and rapid developing business growth? I shall attempt to explain as below:

In fact, it is not essential to any managers or CEOs need to spend time to learn how any why what factors may influence their organizations to grow up to next business life cycle stage, but in comparison one learning how to change organizational life cycle stages manager and non-learning how to change organizational life cycle stages manger. Can learn attitude or strategy to help the manager to develop or expand his organization to next life cycle stage more easily or rapidly? I shall attempt to explain as below:

In fact, any organizations expect to change to next life cycle stage in success , can the manager(s) learn how to implement strategies to achieve to change management to their organizations' development in success? How the organizational management learns how to adapt organizational management change, it may be one important factor to influence whether the organization needs to spend how long time to reach growth life cycle stage from birth stage or reach mature life cycle stage from growth stage. So, it seems that how management spends time to learn how to change his/her organization. It will have relationship to the organization needs to spend long time to reach next life cycle stage successfully.

Hence, learning how to train employees in each life cycle stage, it is the important factor to influence any organizations succeed, the employee lifecycle is an ongoing process that starts and ends with competent employees in any managers' organizations. There are nine elements ofa successful change management process, if the organizational management expects whole organization can real reach to next life cycle stage in success. The nine elements of a successful change management process, any management needs to spend time to learn. They may include: readiness assessments, communication planning implementation, sponsor activities and sponsor roadmaps organizing, organizatons need to provide change management training for managers to learn how to achieve effectiveness as well as providing training development and delivery learning methods to them, resistance management learning and learning employee feedback and corrective action. Moreover, managements also need to spend time to learn change management steps in order solve any challenges in order to reach next life cycle stage easily.

The change management learning steps may include: Step 1: Urgency creation , step 2: Building every team serves to every department efficiently, learning how to create avision, how to communication of division, how to remove obstacles, going for quick wins, let the change mature, integrate the change. These elements are incorporated into change management phases process. For example, some elements of communication planning occur early in the lifecyle. At this stage, change management is not fully achieved effectively, so management needs to spend more time to learn how to achieve effective communication planning in order to achieve effective communication planning in order to keep whose organization employees can communicate to work efficiently. Also, it will help client service employees to know how to build good communication management method to deal or answer or satisfy their clients' sale service and improving service performance absolutely.

Because organizations are nor statis, they change , if one organization still stays long time in birth stage, it represents that the organization feels difficulties to continue develop . So, the management needs to find whether what challenges threaten its organization can not reach growth stage more easily. One failure changing management organization, it has these characteristics: failure to change, inexperienced management, not enough revenue, inadequate leadership. Hence, it has close relationship between employee life cycle and organizational life cycle . If the organizational management expects its organization can continue develop or reaches next life cycle stage in success, it needs to learn how to let employees to adapt when its organization is changing in order to keep efficience and improving service performance absolutely . So, I believe that it has relationship between learning change management and reaching to mature business cycle stage rapid and achieving long time staying in business cycle mature stage .

The question concerns that how management can learn to implement change management strategy in order to let his organization can reach mature cycle stage in short time as well as keep to stay in this mature life cycle stage in long time?

Firstly, we need to know what change management life cycle means ? For information technological industry example, it may be explained that the change management process is designed to help control of the life cycle of strategies, tactical and operational changes to IT services through standardized procedures. The goal of change managent is to control risk and minimize disruption to IT service and business operations. So, IT industry, the process change management maturity model presents five levels of organizational maturity in change management: The five level may include: from the lowest level 1 to the highest level 5, level 1: Absent or Ad hoc, level 2: Isolated projects , level 3: Multiple projects, level 4: Organizatinal standards and level 5: organizational competency. So, for IT , software manufacturing industry, if the management knows how to manage and change software manufacturing quality in order to satisfy manufacturing organization can follow software users' needs to change old function to new function and improve their qualities to achieve the highest level 5 organizational competency level.

Then, I believe that due to this organization's software management can learn how software user needs change and change its any kinds of software functions (software life cycle), when its all softwares can be often changed to more new functions to create many different kinds of new software functions to satisfy software users needs and fight its software competitors in this often changing needs market. Due to software product may experience often changing life cycle stages. So, for often one learning software manager example, I believe that he can help this software organization to reach growth life cycle stage, even mature life cycle stage more easily in short time as well as he can also help his software organization to stay in mature life cycle stage long time if this software organizational manager can keep learning attitude to continue to create any new kinds of different functions software to satisfy software clients' changing needs for long time . Then, I believe that this software organization may experience or reach growth life cycle stage, even mature life cycle stage as well as continue staying long time on mature life cycle stage or avoid to encounter decline life cycle stage occurrence chance, if this software organization's softeare management can learn how to change software organization operation and software manufacture and sale strategy in order to satisfy this software users' needs in this software users' need often changing market . So, it is one example to explain why it has close relationship between learning organizational management method and business life cycle stages. As this software organization case, the software management needs often to create and change any new kinds of software functions in order to satisfy software users' needs . So, the software managers need to spend time to learn software life cycle stage , it can help the software organization may reach products life cycle stage, even mature life cycle stage in short time,even the software product organization may also stay long time in mature life cycle stage , when it can reach this stage. Hence, learning how to change organizational management or strategy, which is one important factor to help any organization can reach growth or mature life cycle stage eadily in short time.

As Lewin describes that the change as a three stage process of unfreezing, change and freezing . In this phases of change model, Lewin emphasizes that change is that a series of individual processes, but rather one that flows from one process to the next . So, in general, services mature firms pace greater emphasis on more bureaucratic form, control systems might need to change throughout the life cycle to fit in with. He explains they have relationship between both organizational life cycle stage and management control.

Effective management control may help the organization to reach mature life cycle in short time rapidly. So, leadership managment and the way of thinking are required to balance control and through several stages of growth, maturity , decline or re-grow changes in the external environment influence. Hence, managers position in each of the stages of life cycle and providing practical solutions are, however world where environment changes have proven a rapid growth, the management of varios , they also need to implement how to change their organizational cultures, strategies in order to let their organizations to reach mature stage with a distinction-oriented rapidly. Hence, to successfully implement change initiatives, for each phase of life cycle. Any organizations need to produce resistance to change (the old model wins out over management boils down to improving the relationship) learning the relationship between leadership style and the organization life cycle were important. The change from one organizational life cycle phase to another, it depends on how the manager'c capacity to learn and change.

However, organizations at any stage of the life cycle are impacted by external environment, for example, threats in the start up stage differ from those in the maturity stage. So, managers must need often to learn when the right time is to be needed to change the goals, instead he also needs to learn types of changes in the maturity stage, comparisons with other, having strong personal and professional relationships in the organizaton's maturity stage. Hence, I believe that it has close relationship between learning change management and reaching maturity life cycle and staying long time in this stage.

● How to achieve the experience of mature life cycle reaching stage rapidly for product and service ?

Any businesses expect they can have chance or possibility to attempt to experience this nature life cycle stage, but it is not guarantee any kinds of businesses must may experience this the topest stage, the question is that: Have any methods may help any kinds of businesses to reach this the topest level of business life cycle, when their businesses had been developing or expanding in a period, e.g. after five years? So, it has no absolute to guarantee any kinds of businesses must may experience this the topest stage in one fixed time. How businesses can adapt to birth and growth life cycle stages in order to reach this the topest mature stage in their business life cycle stages? I shall attempt to explain whether it is possible that achieving what strategies may help businesses bring high successful chance to reach the business life cycle mature stage as below:

Product life cycle with maturity stage, it foucs as an important strategic inflection point. A number of techniques can help their businesses to attempt to reach this stage more easily. In fact, the product life cycle contains four distinct stages: introduction, growth, maturity, and decline. Each stage is associated with changes in the product's marketing position . Any firms can use various marketing strategies in each stage to try to proplong the life cycle of their products.

How do the firm extend the maturity stage of a product? I shall recommend change price , place or promotion extension strategy , what does change price extension strategies mean? Change prices mean proces can be lowered to allow ew customers to buy it as well as change place means that products can be sold in different countries or territories to gain more sales, change promotion means different advertising or sales promotion techniques can proplong the life of the product, giving it a new image. So, any organizations can attempt to achieve this extension strategies in order to adapt in different birth, growth and maturity stages for ther product sale easily. This extension strategies' characteristics is at the product;s price, sold places and promotin methods can be changed in order to adapt clients needs when their products are selling in birth, growth and maturity three stages in order to achieve the most effective sale effort and clients growth increasing for long time.

In fact, any product is like human beings, products also have a limited life-cycle and they pass through several stages in their life cycle. A typical product moves through five stages, namely, introduction or birth, growth, maturity or saturation and decline stages. So, when the product needs the maturity life cycle stage, in this maturity stage, it has these characteristics: The maturity stage of the product life cycle shows that sales will eventually peak and then slow down. During this stage, sales growth has started to slow down, and the product has already reached widespread acceptance in the market, in relative terms, utimately, during this stage, sales will peak . Hence, any businesses ought need to consider what key strategies can be implement to achieve the best sale performance throughout the different product life cycle stages and how to make the most of each stage. For example, when the product is selling in the birth stage, e.g. one author's book , his book is selling to the publisher in the first year, there are not many readers knew this book existence, so this book is not popular, its price ought not change high to compare similar topic book, e.g. story book in this year, but after this year, if there are many readers know this book and readers number can grow up rapidly. This author's this topic story book does not change, either increases or decreases , but its sale number has been significant increasing after the first year . So, this author's this story book ought be raised book price to attempt to sell easily. It is one good example of extension strategy to this author's this story book in its life cycle stages. So, such as ths publisher book sale case, it may attempt to achieve extension strategies to every author's book sale, it can follow every author's book prices, publishing places and promotion methods to help every author to sell in the most competitive book sale price, sale place choice and promotin methods in order to earn their readers growth aim . So, any book , it is as product to book shop, it will experience introduction, growth, and maturity life cycle stages. Some books may attract many readers to consider or some books may not attract many readers to consider to read . So, it causes their reading life cycle stages staying time will be different. So, extension strategies can help any books to be sold easily.

In fact, instead of product has life cycle stage, any service also has life cycle stage. There are five stages in service lifecycle. Thay may include: Service strategy, service design, service transition, service operation and continual servce improvement five stages. The service strategy phase of the service lifecycle provides guidance on how to design , develop and implement service management. Because any service business needs to manage to any employee service performance in order to provide excellent service quality, e.g. property management service to building tenants or property owners , if the peoperty management furm can train employees to provide excellent property management service to let their managing building clients to feel satisfactory. Then, the property management firm ought may keep long time property management service to this building. So, service provider will also experience service performance different stages.

In different service performance life cycle stages, such as this property management service case, they ought implement dfferent strategies in order to let their employees to know how to achieve service performance improvement to let their servicing building clients (tenants or builgin owners) can feel their property management service can be continue improved to avoid to choose any property management service provider to replace it easily.

The purpose of the service strategy stage of the service life cycle is to define the perspective, position plans and pattern that a service provider needs to be able to execute to meet an organization business outomes. The objective of service strategy may include: An understandng of work strategy is thus either the concept of the product life cycle or the concept of the service life cycle is today at about to give a propsed new product or service , how and to what extent. This generally requires important changes in marketing strategies and methods, because any learning kinds of service or product lif cycle stage why and how to change to any organizational management, it may be an important tool for marketers, managers, and product and service providing designers alike, If specifies four individuals stages of a product's or service's life and offers guidance for developing strategies to make the best use of these stages and promote the overall success of the product or service in the marketplace.

Reasons managment needs to spend time to learn how to manage his/her product or service life cycle development stage? They may include: The product or service life cycle is determined by how long its marketable . Product or service life cycle also plays a critical role in marketing strategy . So, learning how to adapt your product or service to meet the coming trends , this is the stage what will occue in which differentiation when the kind of the product or service will have possible to reach the another new experience life cycle stage in order to adapt its business development more easily.

Hence, each stage is associated with changes in the product's or service's marketing postion . The organizational management can use various markting strategies in each stage to try to prolong the life cycle of your products or services . Any product or service reaches the marketplace, it enters the service or product life cycle . This product cycle typically has for stages: Introduction or birth, growth, maturity and decline (and possibly deaths stages for product as well as service strategy stages includes service strategy. service design, servic transition, service operation, and continual service stages four service stages. So, the organization management can spend time to learn how to develop its business product or service needs to change in order to adapt marketing change in its product or service different life cycle stages. It can bring these benefits, such as: true benefits of product or srvice life cycle management may include, reduced time to makret, reduced market entry costs, more efficient and profitable distribution challen, higher return on investment from promotional cappaigns in possible, extending the lifetime of your product or service by adapting your approach as it moves through the lifecycle , for example, any management needs to learn what can make its products or services move from growth to maturity. After the introduction and growth stages, a product or service passes into the maturity stage. IN the first two stages , companies try to establish a market and then grow sales of their product or service to achieve as large , a share of that market as possible. Hence, marketers must be sure that a product or service has moved from one stage to the next before changing its marketing strategy. At each stage, marketing strategy varies. Strategy for the different stages of the product or service life cycle strategies may include: such as more benefits may be provided to the customers, e.g. extending the warranty period, guarantee period etc. However, company's market strategy depends on which stages the product or service is in its life cycle, for example, when one software manufacture company expects to expand its software sale market to overseas from local in growth stage. If it expects that it can reaches maturity stage in short time rapidly. It needs to implement technology innovation strategy for competition advantage reasons in global software sale markets development. Thus, the software organizational manager needs to spend time to learn what its present organizational characteristics are what resources and skills it owns or lacks, that gives it to comparative advantages over different countries to the operating changes that result in the learning curve to prepare this software product sale organizational maturity life cycle stage development more successfully. So, it needs to look at the advantages of focusing on what kinds of software manufacture and sale services in this software development industry whole life cycle stages and find the best or the most suitable competitive straregy, e.g. a discountinuous change to the software product development marketplace, what the global software product development industrial stage is and the tertiary or sale services sector durig the maturity life cycle stage to this softare manufacturer and sale organization strategy to this software firm during this growth stage may include example of it how changed its software product sales channels to which countries will be its another expanding sale market choice.

On conclusion, any organization management ought spend time to learn whether which strategies are the most suitable or the best to implement as well as how to implement when it is experiencing in the prodiuct or life cycle stage in order to spend less time to reach the maturity life cycle stage and proplong its maturity life cycle stage more success.

Organizational life cycle stage decision making strategy

Every company must have strategy to make any important or not important decision. Any decisions must be very important because they may influence any companies' future development. So, our company management can not neglect to cosider whether all strategies are reasonable to influence any organizations success. However, we need to consider how to achieve effective decisions to avoid wrong decisions to cause our companies' development in long term.

The question is how to implement effective decision making to achieve every consequence to gain the best benefits to any organizations? Any organization managers ought need to follow these steps in order to make effective decisions. Acknowledge and compensate for your biases, use positive and negative lists, experiment by reversing your live of thinkin, create a scoring system. Any organizational decisions have four decision making styles. They may include these four basic categories for decion making, these being: Directive, conceptual, consultative, and consensue. So, strategic decisions usually mean managers must plan for change and risk.

Many factors are unknown, since managers are planning for future changes.

Another example for a major change is the decision to modify the company's culture. For instance, the firm may be having trouble with increased employee turnover. It may be the company's culture needs to be changed in order to employees can adapt to work together. Hence, when one company's working environment and employees attidude is poor, because they feel unhappy to work, so working environment will be caused poor. It may be influenced whole organizational culture to be more poor. Hence, the organizational ought need to change its organizational culture to be more happy in order to let whole organization's employees can feel happy to work in this enjoyable working environment . Hence, any entrepreneurs or managers ought need to consider employees' emotion issue how to let they have good working emotion to do their tasks every day, e.g. get comfortable with the cost of deciding , teaching employees hoe to control themselves emotion, understand that logical decisions have a secret emotional intuitive is one of the simplest, and arguably one of the most common ways to make a decision, rational decision making is the type of decision making many people want to believe what they do.

The first stage model to any making strategic decisions, they may include: defining the problem, consider these questions, gathering information, seeking information on how any why the problem occurred, developing and evaluating options, generating a wide range of options, choosing the best action, selecting the option that best meets the decision objective. Hence, decision including strategies are the ways, we use information to make a choice, in this case, managers need to make strategic choices as muually exclusive options, start with the most apparent options, generate alteratives, specify the conditions under which each option is attractive, identify barriers to each option, design and run tests to prove or disprove each of the conditions, finally using the data, make a decision. Hence, business leaders use strategic decision-making when they plan the company's future strategic management involves definingl long term goals, responding to market forces and carrying out the firm's mission, so making strategic decisions managers look at the big picture.

In psychology view, decision making is regarded as the cognitive process , knowledge necessary to know when to use any strategies. They do posses to change their approach to decision making. Rather, think of it is a decision making process that keeps you from making the same mistakes year after year. Making-judgement-based decisions among a variety of variable options is made easier when a systematic process is utilized. So, decision making strategies are the structured method and operational guidelines followed by decision makers. So, any strategic decision making process is needed in the procedural rationality stage, if the organization expects to do the most reasonable decision making to solve any challenges. So, strategic decision making is essential on how top managers use process and tools to implement long-term goals. Also, decision making is a process that reduces uncertainty to a considerable level.

In most decisions, uncertainty will be reduced, when the manager had prepared one good strategic decision making method, the most difficult decison making suitation is that when the manager needs to implement a multi-perspective strategic decision making. It is the process of making long-term decision's that helps or helps the organization t build long term benefits. However, any organization's managers ought need to spend time to learn a large variety of decision making techniques, it can help improve decisions of different types.

It can be useful in decision between strategies or investment opportunities with constrained resources. This is called strategic decision making, where decisions are made according to a company's goals or mission. At many organizations, it is up to managers to make the key decisions that influence business strategy. So, managers must need to learn how to implement any kinds of strategic decision making method in order to help their organizations to achieve the most reasonable long term benefits. However, with any strategic planning process, any organization will be able to know. What it wants to achieve in the long term vision is on ongoing process that involves crafting strategies to achieve goals.

● Why do managers feel difficult to make decisions?

Usually these factors may cause managers feel difficult to make decision for their organizations: Making decisions will always be difficult because it takes time and energy to weigh their options. Things like second-guessing the manager himself/herself and feeling indecisive and just a part of the process. However, decision-making is important to achieve the organizational goals/objectives within given time and budget. It searches the best alternative, utilizes the resources properly and satisfies the employees at the workplace. As a result, organizational goals or objectives can be achieved as per the desired result. Moreover, decision-making is an integral part of modern management.

Decisions play important roles as they determine both organizational and mangerial activities. A decision can be defined as a consequence of action purposely chosen from a set of alternatives to achieve organizational or managerial objectives or goals. The first step to making those decision is understanding what makes managers themselves so hard, the decisions that may include senior leaders, middle managers, frontline staffs , they many face short time or long time decision making challenge , when they need to find solution methods to solve any organizational challenges. For example, one manager needs to make decision to resolve organizational challenge before tomorrow morning time. Then, time pressure can lead to poor decision making to influence the manager feels physically, mentally ad personally pressure. He will have much chance to make poor decisions when he feels he is in a position of power. IF he can not make any decisions to help his organization to solve challenge before tomorrow morning, he will not achieve any satisfactory management effort to the company's senior management, even CEO . So, time pressure may be one main factor to cause the manager to do poor decision making to help his organization to solve the challenge.

So, if the manager hopes to make better decision making , he needs likely feel comfortable and confident making decisions, e.g. learning how to manage his senior manager or CEO expectations. However, some decisions carry enough weight that the prospect of simply making a choice can be made in short time. SO, the manager ought need to learn how to weight whether which choices may bring more benefits or advantages ro make any decision in short time frequently every day. It can train that when the manager encounter difficult problem to be solved in short time. He can be trained to judge whether which is the most suitable choice easily to do any decision more easily. So, daily learning how to solve any short time or long time decision making skill frequently, this learning behavior must help any managers to raise short time critical thinking decision making skilful effort. Hence, learning managing uncertainty and making the most reasonable choices , strategic decision making skill, it will be any organizational managers ought need to consider issue if they want to be the best strategic decision maker in themselves organizations.

Hence, any organizational managers need to know that decision making is difficult to taugh, particularly when there may not be one right answer. It's common for managers and leaders to feel alone. Being alone as a decision maker comes with the job. However, decision making is absolute one of the toughest parts of running a business. They will feel responsible for it, compared to the management announcing the change in policy without listening to what. Hence, self confidence, time management factor, is a important part to influence any managers to do any important decision making more success. So, they can not neglect how to train themselves to attempt to find the most reasonable decision making to solve any chalenges for themselves organizations in order to achieve one strategic decision maker for their organizations.

On conclusion, managers' attitudes toward work and incentives may influence his decision making whether it can be more accurate, when reviewing upon motivation, incentives, the social psychology of work and behavior at work, it is tempting to conclude that managers are motivated when manual workers need bonus payment, between ideas , beliefs attitudes. So, any managers individual personal attitudes will influence their behaviors, also his behaviors will motivate how he can make resonable decision making. So, manager's working attitude can be one factor to influence whether his/her decision making can be made more reasonable for his/her organization.

Computer technologic firm merger cooperational strategy

● IBM and Apple merger strategic advantages and disadvantages

IBM and Apple computer firms, they merger to cooperate together, whether merger will help them to bring what advantages and disadvantages ? What is the life cycle stage to these two big computer organizations? These two computer companies IBM and Apple , they had set up abut forty years. From 1970 year, when Apple founders, they had invented new computer machine to bring human playing electronic game to entertain at home. Then, IBM founder also invented micro softword clerical software to let any office workers or students or home users can type on computers to replace typing machines . So, Micro soft word software invention also help office workers or students or home users to choose to apply computer to do typing tasks to replace traditional typing machines. So, these two firms' borth stage, is that when Apple desktop computer products are innovated as well as Microsoft IBM micro soft word softwares are also innovated to this traditional typing market.

When, 1980, there are not that Microsoft word softare functions are, so these two founders will spend long time to promote desktop computers and microsoft word software new products to let many people know what their real functions are, e.g. playing electronic entertainment game activities and clerical tasks , these two main functions to let them to know, when they may be known whether what microsoft word software and Apple brand desktop computer can help any students or clerical office workers or home users to do any clerical tasks or play electronic playing game leisure activites at homes or offices. Then , many people begin to accept these both new products to use for their daily clerical tasks or electronic playing game lesiures activies .

However, in their birth life cycle stage time needs about two years short time only, because their advesrtisement strategies are effective to let global many people feel computer product can belp us to fo any clerical tasks or bring exciting electronic playing game leisure feeling when students feel bore, they may spend some times to apply computer to play any games at homes. Even they may turn on computers to apply Microsoft word sofware to help them to do any homeworks or assignments. Students can use computers to replace typing machines to type any clerical documents at homes or schools conveniently.

After1982 year, global IBM computer and Microsoft word software buyers number had been increasing rapidly. So, from 1982 year, these two firms are experiencing life style growing stage period. Till to 1988 year, these two firms may ensure global computer and software products main suppliers their computer and software technological products had high market share. So, in global computer and software technological market, these are not many competitors to win them. So, they do not need long time to enter life cycle growing stage. They only need four ro five years time to attract many global computer and software buyers begun to accept their products and also choose to buy their IBM and Microsoft computers and softwares to use. Hence, then 1988 year, these two high technolgical computer and software product firms had been experiencing life cycle mature stage till to 2000. Although, in this forty , IBM and Apple computer firms number had been increasing rapidly globally. But, other computer and software competitors number is also increasing, e.g. Dell computer brand had be familiar to global computer buyers. Dell's market share is also high. So, their computer and software buyers may have many kinds of computers and softwares brands of product choices in global students and office clerical workers and home users computer and software product market.

In fact, IBM and Apple began to enter life cycle decline stage , due to laptop products need increase and many different brands of laptop computers may be supplied to let computer users to choose to buy in global computer market. So, after 2000 , these two computer firms began to change to new technologial product or service market, e.g. apply also invented Smart mobile products because it felt desktop and laptop products competitors number had been decreasing , due to they had many laptops and desktops competitors' products to choose to buy. So, Apple brand computer begun to invent smart mobile phone and small flat laptop , it has or has none phone function products in order to earn high market share to smart mobile and flat laptop product user market ratio in order to avoid life cycle decline stage reachs rapidly.

In fact, IBM smart mobile strategy may be effective to absord global some smart mobile customers. But IBM is skill desktop same smart mobile competitors. Also, IBM laptop and desktop products may also face different similar computer function products to choose from competitors.So, IBM will may enter life cycle decline stage rapidly. Also, Microsoft brand computer may be its main competitor, Microsoft can attempt to apply interest technology to help it to sell electronic book, because it felt desktop and laptop product market has reached mature stage.

It is common that global every family had own at least one laptop or desktop or both computer product. So, it means that product needers number begins to decrease, when global every family own at least one computer product to use at home, even global every office also wn at least one computer in offices. Unless, their computers are broken , thwy ill feel need to buy another new. Otherwise, they use computers about three to five years when they feel too old,then they will choose to change another new. So, Microsoft applies internet to help it to sell electronic book, it can bring another electconic publish business chance, instead of selling laptop, desktop, Microsoft software products only, because it also feel that when computer market had reached mature period. Global many people had owned computers, their needs will also decrease. Since internet invention, it creates e-commerce chance, electronic publishing is also popular to let global readers to read any books from desktop or laptop computers or mobile computers tools anywhere. So, Microsoft is attempting to enter this electronic publish market . this electronid publishing reading service market does not need readers to buy paper books to read, they won't need feel heavy if they need to bring bags to carry many heavy books to go to schools, libraries , students only need to bring laptops to read any Microsoft publish electonic books from computers anywhere conveniently. So, Microsoft electronic book pubishing new market help it to avoid to experience the life cycle decline stage rapidly. But, these two firms are still main competitors , if they choose not to merger or coopeerate to do technologic product, e.g. laptop, desktop , software or electronic book publish online reading service together. They may influence their clients number to reduce. Otherwise, if they can merger or cooperate , then it is possible that their clients nu,ber may increase or profit increase, even fight other computer and software companies competitors easily. Then, their computer and softare market share may raise when other competitors number reduces, e.g. Dell may be their main computer competitor, but if they cooperate or merger , then Dell's clients may be influenced to choose to buy their any desktops, laptops, softwares products. They can help themselves invention high technological products , if they can attribute their unique computer technology to help to invent any new kinds of more advanced computers or softwares , e.g. even high technological electronic reading platform to be improved to publish high reading quality of electronic books to attract many readers to read their electronic books from their publishing webstores.

IBM and Microsoft merger or cooperation can help them to raise market share or fight competitors in this often changing high technological computer product market. What are the disadvantages and advantges when they choose to merger or cooperate together? I shall explain as below:

Can IBM and Microsoft merger can keep their computer , software , even electronic book publish market in the mature life cycle stage in long time in order to avoid decline life cycle stage occurs. IBM's global strategy is based on three aspects: cloud , data and engagement . IBM's strategy imperatives may is business growth on cloud, analytics, mobile, social and society . So, it has changed its old strategy only concentrates on computer sold aspect. Since internet technology had been invented. However, IBM's primary generic strategy is cost leadership.

In Michael Porter's model, the generic strategies are what companies use to ensure competitive advantages . The cost leadership generic competitive strategy supports IBM's competitive advantages through cost-effectiveness of its operaton. However, if IBM can operate or merger to Microsoft, then Microsoft ought may help it to reduce more cost , when their technology can assist to develop their products, e.g. IBM's clouds , data technologic strengths can be brought to Microsoft 's product or Microsoft's electronic book publishing technology or software manufacturing technology strengths can bring to IBM' s products to assist themselves to raise computer, smartphone phoe, electronic publishing reading technological service business competitive effort in global computer , smartphone and electronic book publish markets. Then, when IBM can own Microoft 's technology , it may help it to reduce manufacturing cost in possible.

In fact, instead of IBM may merger to microsoft to reduce its cost to be more. It may also merger to Amazon, Amazon is us one online electronic book sale provider, it help global different businesses to apply itself online platform to sell their products. It is middleman role, it helps any sellers to sell their products from its online store platform. Any one can turn on computer and click to Amazon website to buy any products . Amazon will help any buyers to deliver their products to their homes by flight , after they pay visa card, because Amazon is global the topest online product sale service middleman provider. It's cloud technology is very proficient. If Amazon and IBM can merger to cooperate to do themselvers cloud service high technological business. IBM can apply Amazon's cloud high technological platform to help itself to grow its business and increase its cloud service clients number more easily. So, IBM ought choose Amazon's cloud platform to assist itself to continue to develop its future cloud service business, e.g. electronic book publish, because Amazon's electronic book publish market has have high reading market share.

Hence, IBM needs to find, e.g. Amazon or Microsoft to expand its high technological product or cloud strategy or cloud technology may be IBM's main competitors. If Amazon and IBM and Microsoft can merger or cooperate to expand themselves unique computers or softwares ot smart mobiles or electronic book platform sale markets to be merger together, then global computer buyers , smart mobiles buyers , electronic book readers, electronic platform product buyers must may enjoy the most benefits, because they can attribute their unique computers, smart mobiles manufacture, cloud service platform technology to be applied to themselves unique computers, smart mobiles, electronic book reading flatform and ebooks ale mix together, t means to improve these products or services unique function or improve themselves technology in order to let global computer , smart mobile or electronic book readers or electron platform product buyers feel that their these products or cloud platform products sale or reading service performance can br improved. Hence, their merger ought bring advandages more than disadvantages.

However , I shall also indicate some possible disadvantages to IBM merger strategy. Higher prices to IBM products, A merger can reduce competition and give the IBM more monopoly power with less competition and greater market share to IBM, but when IBM chooses to merger to Micrsoft and / or

IBM chooses to merger to MIcrosoft and/or Amazon , they may influence IBM's computer or smartmobile phone products can usually increase prices for consumers. Then, consumers may also compare IBM's products to other computer and smart mobile phone sellers. If they feel its price is not reasonable, they may choose to buy other smart mobiles or choose to buy other brands of laptops, desktops to replace IBM's product. Because IBM's any products prices may be controlled or dominated by Microsoft or Amazon after they merger. So, IBM can not change itself products prices more easily. It is its weaknesses . Another risk's associated with mergers and acquisitions to IBM, it may be differences in culture between Amazon and Microsoft and IBM. It may bring inefficient communication and lack of transparency to IBM organization when Amazon and Microsoft staffs may participate to IBM any important decisions. It may bring miscalculations in the evaluation of assets to IBM. For example, merger may bring disadvantages when the main drivers behind the Lenovo and IBM merger. The drivers behind the merger between China's Lenovo and US IBM was inspired by several moves. The main one being the loss that the latter incurred to IBM itself pc division after a change of business strategy.

On conclusion , before IBM decides to implement merger strategy to any technological firms, it needs to consider whether what risks they may bring and what benefit they may bring after IBM itself chooses to merger to the firm in order to avoid miscalculation consequence to influence IBM's business continues to develop or reachs life cycle decline stage rapidly.

CHAPTER THREE

Technology or human behavior influences economy development

Human Behavioral network job brings social economic benefits

What does human network job mean ? Why may human network job be popular? Why human network job behavior may influence economy ? Nowadays internet is popular to use. We can apply internet to find data , search any new things, even earn money. Why does internet may become huma network job source. For example, e-publish may be one kind of new human network job. Any authors may apply internet channel to help them to sell electronic or paper books from e-publisher web store. They may apply facebook, you tub etc. any online channel to promote themselves new books to let new readers to know whether when they may buy themselves favourable new topic books to read

from electronic publisher web store.

Thus, future electronic publisher industry may help any authors to build internet network platform to help them to sell and promote ot advertise their any one new electronic or paper book topic to let global any one reader to choose to buy their any new topic books from electronic publisher web store easily and conveniently. However, it implies that electronic network platform author may be one kind of future new human network job in our societies.

How electronic network platform author job may bring economy benefit in macro economy view? A person can have few friends, contacts and still be very influential if these few

friends and contacts are themselves highly influential, e.g. one author must not need to know any one reader in global society. When they like to choose any electronic books from electronic internet network platform. They may become the author's any one topic book buyer, when they feel the author's any one topic book is fun and attract they make decision to buth the strange author whose the topic book from electronic book publisher's platform web store conventiently in short time. Although, they are strangers, they do not know themselves , but the reader can understand what it way that made Google from writing platofrm to create new creative mind and typing network job method to replace traditional hand writing book method for global authors. It will be one kind of new human network writing job.

Hence, global any one reader can apply an innovative search engine , such as google.com to find whether whom author personal new topic books are value to read from internet.

Then, the electroniuc publisher's web store may be new book store platform sale network to help the author to sell many electronic or paper books from electronic network platform

in short time. So, internet may be future new network plaform to help global any one author to create network writing job absolutely. Furthermore, internet may be popular social media

to help any one author to build goold relationship between his/her readers. It is one kind of new network, human network job. New authors do not need to buy many paper books to prepare to put in any one book shop warehouse. Their every book can print on demand to reduce out of book stock in any one book shop. They may choose to sell either electronic books or paper books both from any one book publisher web store. So, electronic network platform may be one kind of good writing channel to help human authors to create income and it can also help authors to bring new creative mind and new topic fun content books to let readers to know and buy to read from electronic publisher network platform.

Why does human behavior may be one kind of new human network job to bring global economic advantages. ALthough, it may be free income or without inocme, but the person does the network behavior, his/her behavior may be bring advantages to influence many other people's health. For this case, when a worker in a coffee shop in an airport gets a vaccination aganinst the flu, it does not only helps him or her stay healthy, but also helps the many travellers who might otherwise have been inflected if that workers caught the flu. So, the externality , the result implies the vaccination of even a part of a community conveys benefits to the whole community. For example, governments pay special attention to the vaccinations of school children, teachers, health mothers, and the elderly, categories of people particularly susceptible not only to catching, but also to transmitting a disease.

It is not accidential that governments are heavily involved with vaccination . When there are externalities, free market, fail to persuade individual incentives with society's
their the worker's decision of whether to get a vaccine ends up attracting whether other people get sick. The workers might not fully take all these other people's potential suffering into account when making her or his vaccination decision.

As Stanford University does many suggestions, understand this and tries to help them make the right decisions and so providers free flu vaccines for its staff and students.
Small pockets of unvaccinated individuals can allow a disease to gain a spread more widely well-being. For example, parent weighing the costs and benefits of a vaccine for their child is not always thinking of the consequences of that vaccination to other people. THese are markets in which subsidizing or regulating behavior can make everyone better off. Because the reason for requiring that a child be vaccinated before enrolling in school is not just to protect that child, because each child's vaccination affects others via potential contagions.

Robots take our jobs behavioral and economy influences
Robot job behavior brings economy influences

If one day robots can replace human to do simple, even complex jobs. They will bring what influences to our global societial economy.The popular economic refrain declares that the
global middle class is dying and robots will soon take our jobs, e.g. shopping center customer service jobs, library service jobs, cinema ticket sale jobs, restaurant kitchen cooker jobs,
even, bus drivers, taxi drivers etc. public transport driving jobs, accountant, doctors etc. professional jobs. Whether it is beautiful or petty matter if our future societies have many human jobs can be replaced to do from robots.

Businessman must may reduce to employ employees and reduce to pay salary or wage, when robots can be replaced to do their employees tasks. But, societies must bring unemployement rate rises , due to societies will have many people loss jobs when their employers choose to buy robots to serve their clients or do any office tasks or customer service or cleaning etc. tasks.

In micro economy view, employers may save money in long term, but in macro economy view, it will cause unemployment ratio rises , even crime rate rises when there are many people lose
jobs in societies. These models of doom, though, fail to account for the hundreds of businesses riding the waves of change in their industries when robots may be invented to replace human to do many simple , even complex tasks in our future societies.

WE may image that one small factory needs to manufacture fishes canes to sell to supermarket, the small , cheaper stuff and higher margin parts of the fishes manufacture industry. Before, this factory needs to employe many human factory workers need to help every fresh customer makeing the perfect fishing gear, designed for performance, durability, and cost in order to achieve to manufacture every fish cane in whole fished processing manufacturing stages. Every worker needs to spend about 15 to twenty minutes to finish every fish cane , till to delivery to any supermarket to sell. If this fish canes manufacturing factory can apply manufacturing robots to help them to finish any one working tasks , every robot can only spend five minutes to finish whole fresh fish cane manufacturing process. Thus, every robot can
help this factory save 10 to 15 minutes time to finsh every fish cane manufacturing process. IN fact, time is money, because when every robot can help this factory to reduce 10 to 15 minutes time to compare human worker. Then, this factory can finish about 20 fish canes in one hour if it can use robot to help it to manufacture fish canes. Otherwise, if this factory still use human workers to help it to manufacture fish canes, then it can finsh about 3 to 4 fish canes in one hour. SO, the manufacturing efficiency ensures that robots must help this fish manufacturing factory to raise fish canes number more than human workers. So, in robotic behavioral economy view, manufacturing robots must help this fish canes manufacturing factory to raise fish canes manufacturing number and deliver increasing number to supermarkets to prepare to sell every day. Robots can help this fish canes manufacturing factory bring manufacturing time saving,

rising manufacturing efficiency, improving performance and reducing wages expenditure long time advantages in micro economy view. However, manufacturing robots can also bring disadvanages to society, e.g. increasing unemployment ratio, increasing crime rate,
this factory workers will lose jobs and income, they need earn social welfare from government and increasing government finance pressure in short time, even long time in macro economic view.

Stanford University graduate program in economics, Scott lecturer explained that "in demand and supply economic theory for robots supply and demand case, robots supply number increasing may influence human workers demand number decrease. It sometimes calls " the efficient frontier".

No specific human beings were mentioned in any of economics classes. As robots supply and demand in market case, They (robots) may be purely theoretical " agents" who reached to the most reasonable sale prices in order to persuade any one businessman buyer to make manufacturing robot buying decision whether robots can help him / her to bring how much saving time , saving money, saving cost, improving performance, efficiency economic benefit before he/she plans to reduce workers number when he/she decides to apply robots to replace human workers in his/her factory or office or any service department, e.g. cinema ticket sale service, shopping center customer service, shopping center cleaning , supermarket customer service etc. service or sale tasks. When robots can replace human to do any one of these tasks in any organizations. So, robots may be human worker agents who reached to prices the way robots would react to a software
command. There was nothing that explained why some people thrived and others did n't or why truly brilliant, hardworking people could fail when much lazier folks succeeded." Having been admitted to the Stanford University graduate program in economics, Scott lecturer hoped to get his answers there.

How robots influence our future social changing? Using the right technology can be a boon to your business in this economy. For internet example, it is easier than ever to find well-matched customers all around the world, to stay in contact with them, and to more quickly design the products they want. If you focus solely on being cutting -edge, though you risk letting the technology
take over what should be very robust relationships with your customers , employees, and colleagues. IN nowaddays society, technoligical advances

and cutomation, personal

relationships in business are more crucial than ever. I mean that robots can not replace human to serve clients to let them to feel more comfortable and passion more easily. For shoe shop case example, if the shoe shop apply one robot to serve its clients to replace human shoe salesperson to serve its shoe customers. Robots ensure that they can not persuade every shoe potential buyer to make shoe buying decision more easily when robots need to contact every shoe potential buyer. The reason is simple, because robots can not touch any one shoe buyer individual emotion very easier.

If the shoe buyer needs the robots to help him/her to choose any right shoe styles when he/she can not feel himself / herself can make the most right shoe style choice decision. The robots can not replace human shoe salesperson to make shoe style choice judgement more easily. They must need longer time to analyze whether which shoe style may be the most suitable to the shoe buyer. Otherwise, human shoe salesperson may attempt to make the most right shoe style choice decision to help any one shoe buyer to chooce the most right style shoe because he/she owns shoe style sale experience, shoe style knowledge, the most important reason is that they can feel every shoe customer individual emotion to touch whether he/she will feel comfortable or happy when they attempt to help every shoe customer to seek the most right shoe style in every shoe customer whole shoe searching processing. Othwerwise, serving robots are only one machine, they can not touch or feel every shoe customer individual emotion whether he/she feel comfortable or unhappy or happy when they need to contact them in whole shoe searching processing. Hence, I believe that some tasks robots can

not repalce human staff to do very easily. Otherwise, robots may bring disadvanatges to let any one businessman to loss his/her customers, due to robots can not touch every customer

emotion to compare human staff in service tasks more easily. Robots serving customer behaviors may cause money lose and customers number lose to the shop in micro economic view.

Intellectual human economic behaviors

What does intellectual human economic behaviors mean ? I believe that when we choose or decide to do intellectual behaviors, then our societies will be influenced to bring economic growth in consequence.I shall attempt to indicate pollution case to explain how and why eithet our intellectual or foolish behaviors may bring economic growth or recession in consequence as below:

On one hand, for air pollution social case aspect example, if we only consider to buy cars to drive for working aimr or holiday leisure aim. Then, our societies air will be polluted. Our health will be influenced to bad. Our car driving behaviors may cause global environment air pollution serously. In long tiem, global air pollution will bring our bodies health to be bad. Although, ourselves car driving behaviors may bring our driving travelling leisure enjoyment and comfortable feeling in short time, also we so not need to pay public transport fare often, but we need to compensate ourselves health economic intangible loss due to air pollution , when cars number increases, dirty air will cause ouselves health to become bad.

In the result, we will need to pay more medical expenditure when we are old age, due to ourselves bodies will become bad, due to we breathe global dirty air every day, due to ourselves cars pollute air in long time, e.g. 10 to 20 years, even 30 more without limited air pollution environment. So, driving cars behavior may be one kind of human foolish behavior and our foolish behavior may bring ourselves future long time medical expenditure absolutely.

One the other hand, water pollution social aspect, if we often keep much rubblish to pollute sea, oil exploration porcessing pollute ocean , ships gas pollute ocaen, then fishes will eat polluted food and drive dirty water, due to global ocean is polluted.

In fact, because human only to conside how to buy boats to carry on leisure enjoyment activities, or catch cruises to travel on the sea. Also, oil manufacturers only consider researching anywhere to find new oil exploration places to manufacture oil product, when their oil exploration processes pollute ocarn . Consequently, global fishes drink polluted warer or eat polluted food. They will have poison. SO, human will have high chance to eat poison polluted fishes, due to fishes are poison or are polluted.

So, human is doing foolish activities, we only hope to find oil exploration places to pollute ocean or we only spend money to buy ticket to catch ships to travel anywhere in global ocean. All of these human foolish behaviors will bring pollution to global ocean. On consequently, we will need to compensate to eat polluted or dirty or poision fishes, ourselves bodies health will be bad. In long time, we need have high chance to pay medical expenditure when we are old. So, pollution case may be one good example to explain how and why human foolish behavior may influence ourselves future need to compensate serious medical loss.

All of these human foolish behavior will bring pollution to global ocean. On consequently, we will need to compensate to eat polluted or dirty or poison fished , ourselves bodies health will be bad. In long time, we will have high chance to pay medical expenditure, when we are old. So, pollution case may be one good example to explain how and why human ourselves intellectual or foolish behaviors may influence future long time economic loss or economic growth or recession in micro and micro economic view.

On another water pollution aspect hand, if we often keep rubbish to sea, oil exploration processing pollutes ocean and ships' gas pollute ocean, then fishes will eat polluted food and drink dirty water, due to fishes will eat polluted food and drink dirty sea water because the global ocean is polluted seriously.

In fact, because human only consider how to buy boats to carry on any leisure water activities, or catches cruises to travel on the sea. Also, oil manufacturers only consider any where to find oil exploratin places to manufacture oil products from ocean, when their pol exploration processes can plooute ocean. Consequently, global fishes drink polluted water or eat direty food. They will have poison. So, human will have high chance to eat poison fishes.

Otherwise, such as pollutin case, it can infuence inflation or deflation. Consequently, the reason indicates supply and demand theory. If air pollution is serious, then we will consider health issue, global cars demand number may be influenced to reduce, when global cars number demand will reduce, global car prices and supply number will need to change to fall down in order to attract or persuade global car consumers choose to make car purchase decision.

Hence, global car manufacture number and car price will be influenced to reduce, due to global air pollution issue. Consequently, deflation will occur because when the country citizen usually does not spend much extra saving money to buy car expensive goods. Money value will be low. Otherwise, if global cair pollution is not serious, human considers to buy cars to enjoy driving leisure lives. So, global car demand is influenced to increase , also global car price will also influenced to increase.

Consequently, gobal human will choose to buy cars to drive. Due to we accept to spend extra saving to buy expensive car goods. Car sale price and supply may be influenced to rise up. Money value is influenced to reduce. Inflation may be influenced, due to global car consumers number increases, we would not have extra money to spend easily. Car expensive goods expenditure influences our spending habit to avoid to make car purchase decision more easily. So, human intellectual or foolish activities may bring inflation or deflation consequency in possible indirectly in macro economic view.

On conclusion, above pollution case explain that how and why human intellectual or foolish economic behaviors may bring inflation or deflation consequency as wll as economic growth or recession consequency as well as any goods demand and supply increasing or decreasing consequency. It implies that human behavior may have indirect relationship to influence any goods demand and supply number to either increase or decrease result as well as any goods price will be influenced to increase or decrease in micro and macro economic view.

The relationship between social change and human behavior

Why does economic changes may influence human individual behavioral change? I shall attempt to indicate shopping behavior and staying at home behavior to explain their case and effect relationsip as below:

Human behavior can be influenced by economic change or economic change can be influenced by human behavior? Why does recession may influence consumers reduce shopping desire? In social recession suitation, it is possible that many people lose jobs suddenly, due to businessmen lose many customers. They need to make decision to reduce employees number in order to continue to keep businesses. Consequently, many firms (organizations) their employees may lose jobs. When they have much time, due to lose jobs, they will feel to avoid to spend too much time and money to go to shopping often. Many losing jobs people, they will often stay at homes. So, they will reduce time to go to shopping, then non essential products won't their preferable choice purchase products. Hence, recession will change many losing jobs people their shopping or consumption desires to avoid to buy non essential products often . Usually when economic boom, many people have jobs to do because consumers number must increase when many people have jobs to do. Then, many people can accept to spend money to buy non essential products often. Many people feel spend time to go to shopping can satisfy their purchase of any kinds of new products useful psychology or desire. So, recession is one good example to explain it can influence many people do not like often to leave homes to go to shopping easily. Many people like to stay at homes, becaue they feel worry about spending too much shopping time when they leave homes. Their staying home time is one good negative shopping behavior example. So, economic change may influence human individual behavior changes , they have direct cause and efect relationship in behavioral economic view.

May human behavior influence economic change? Is it possible that human behavior may bring the country social economic change in macro economic or micro behavioral economic view ? I shall indicate publishing industry example. Do you feel that if there are many students feel learning is very important when they read many books or many of students feel interesting to read or they have reading new books in habit, then it is possible that the country will have many students like to spend time to go to any book shops to choose the books, they feel that they can help they learn new knowledge. Then the country will increase students number, they often spend time to visit any one book shop every week. Their visiting book shops behavior which may become their habits. So, the country will increase students number, they often spend time to visit book shops. Also, it implies that visiting book shops behaviors may be their behavioral habits.

So, when the country has many students often spend time to visit book shops , their visiting book shops behaviors may help any one book shop to raise books sale chance. So, the country's student individual often visiting book shop behaviors, their habitual visiting book shops behaviors must may assist help any one book shop to increase books sale number absolutely.

Consequently, any one book shop , its books sale bumber must be influenced to increase to increase because the country will have many students like or feel need visit book shops habit in order to choose any suitable books to buy to read at home in order to raise themselves learning effort. When the country has many bok shops often have many students visit their book shops, then their books sale number may be influenced to increase. It explain why student individual visiting book shop behavior may help any one book shop sale number increases also.

How human productive behavior may influence economic development

May any country which citizen behavior assist themselves country development? It is one cause and effect economic question. I mean that if the country itself citicen can not concentrate mind or energy to choose to do one kind of industry in order to let themselves country can bring the most benefit, then whether the counry itself economy can bring the most serious economic benefit. I shall attempt to indicate these countries themselves indistry choice to explain whether these countries themselves citizen productive behavior may help themselves countries to achieve the largest economic benefits. I shall indicate as below:

New Zealand farmer individual wine productive behavior

For New Zealand country example, this country concerns itself effort is foucs on farming agricultural aspect. So, this country has many farmers concentrate on farming agricultural aspect. May New Zealanders choose to spend time to produce different kinds of wines, e.g. wine or red grape wine is for the people are eating meat, or they are eating dinner.

When these New Zealanders their behaviors choose to do farming or agriculture to grow and produce different kinds of taste of white or red grape wine drinking products job. Themselves grape agriculture behavior will influence these New Zealanders themselves, they can learn how to improve different kinds of grape wine drinking products in order to achieve every kinds of white or read grape wines taste improving aim during their white or red grape producing process.

Why can New Zealander every individual white or read grape wine producers improve their white or read grape wine taste more easily? In behavioral economic view, it can explain that why any one New Zealander white or read grape wine producer can be encouraged or excited or persuaded to concentrate nervous and energy and effort to learn how to improve their white or red grape wine products easily.

In fact, New Zealand is one agricultural food export country. It has good natural environment resource , e.g. land, seed to provide any one farmer to produce themselves any kinds of agricultrual food products, e.g. fruit, or wine food products. Because New Zealanders know themselves country has enough natural resource . So, in common, many New Zealanders choose to attempt to do farming agricultural jobs in order to export themselves any kinds of fruit or meat or wine products to overseas or sell to domestic in order to earn profit.

So, when these New Zealand farmers number has been increasing every year. This country farmers will feel themsleves competition between this New Zealand farmers themselves are serious due to they may feel New Zealanders choose to do agriculture businesses in order to export themselves different kinds of farming food to overseas or sell to local to earn profit.

Hence, when many New Zealand farmers feel that farmers number has been increasing every year. They will feel themselves competition is serious. They must need to spend much time and nervous and effort to research what method is the best how to produce the best taste of white or red grape wine products in order to let local or overseas wine buyers to choose to buy his/her producing white or read grpae products to drink.

Hence, in competition psychological view, may influence many New Zealand white or reaad wine producers had been beginning to change their learning behavior on researching what method is the best in order to produce the best quality of taste red or white wine products to sell in order to attract overseas or local white or read grape wine drinkers to choose to buy his/her wine products. Their behavior will focus on learning how to raising or improving white or read grape wine taste method more than only focus on producing a large number white or red grape wine products. They believe wine quality is more important to compare wine producing number. So, New Zealand wine producers themselves wine producers behaviors have been changing on concentrating on researching wine quality method aspect more then wine producing number aspect in behavioral economic view.

America high technological productive behavior

For America example, US is one high technological country, it owns many high technological knowledge talent inventors, e.g. computer science inventors. Hence, US must attract many diferent countries owning high technological computer inventors choose to go to US to develop their computer science profession career. Also, it seems that when many computer science inventors or professions choose to go to US to develop themselves computer science new career. In behavioral economic view, due to their leaving themselves countries choice, which may bring influence themselve country job behaviors need to be changed. They must need to adapt US new live. Because they will forgive their past computer science job. These computer science professionals need to spend time to adapt US new lives. They " past computer science job behaviors" will need to be changed to their new US any computer employer's new computer science job model.

Because their traditional computer science jobs needed to be forgot in their themselves countries. They will feel their old computer science job knowledge and behavior needed to change in order to let their US any one new of computer company employer feels satisfactory to accept their new working behavior in any one US computer organization.

So, on the other hand, many US computer company employer will feel that they must need time to accept any one new overseas computer science professions their working behaviors, their working attitude daily, because these foreign comouter science professional, their past computer working behaviors and working attitude must be different to US domestic computer science professions.

In behavioral economic view, these overseas computer science professions, their working behaviors and attitude must be needed to change in order to adapt any one US new computer company itself domestic or local computer science professional stafs themselves daily working behaviors and attitude because these overseas and local computer science professionals must need to team work together.

In behavioral economic view, it is only one way that foreign computer science professionals must need to change themselves past country traditiona daily working behaviors and attitude in order to cooperate with these US local computer science professionals in teams more easily.

Consequently, if these foreign compute science professionals can change their past working behaviors and attitude to let any one US local computer science professional feels to cooperate with them easily in short time. Then, the US computer company itself whole computer professional teams themselves efficiencies will be influenced to raised or improved by the changing past working attitude and working behaviors of these foreign computer science professionals. So, in behavioral economic view, only if US any one computer company hopes itself computer teams themselves efficiency can be raised or improved when it decides to employ foreign computer science professionals and US domestic computer science professionals. They need to work in teams together. They must need to let these foreign computer science professionals to know how to change their working behaviors and attitude to let their domestic computer science professionals feel easy to work together. Then, the US computer company itself whole team efficiency must be rasied or improved easily in short time.

● China share market investing behavior

For China share market example, economic development depends on financial market. Because if many Chinese have interest to invest to carry on shares buying and selling activities in orde to learn how to earn shares interest and share profit when the China shareholder can make decision to sell himself/herself shares in the the high price, then he/she can earn money when he/she can sell the China company's shares in the high sale share price position.

If China has many Chinese like to spend time to carry on investing shares activities. Themselves shares buying and selling behaviors will influence

China has many companies can increase fund from many Chinese shareholders in order to have enough money to expand or develop themselves businesses in China in long term.

Consequently, when China can have many Chinese like to attempt to carry on buying and selling shares investing behaviors in China share market. Themselves buying and selling shares behaviors can help many Chinese companies have effort to increase enough money or capital in order to continue to do their businesses in long term absolutely. So, it explains why when many Chinese become shareholders , they can assist China will have many companies continue to develop their businesses if many Chinese like to carry on shares buying and selling investing behaviors in long time in China financial investment market nowadays in behavioral economic view.

Why has any individual country have many people invest share behavior which can influence the country's macro consumption desire?

I shall apply shares market buying and selling investment behavior to explaiin why shares investment behavior which may impact the country's overal consumption desire as below:

In behavioral economic view, I assume that when the coutry has many people have interest to attempt to carry on shares buying and selling investment behavior, then their frequent shares buying and selling behaviors which may bring negactive consumption desire or shopping desire of these shares investors their consumer behavior.

The reason is simple, when the country has many share buyers number suddenly been increasing rapidly. Consequently, these large group share investors must need to spend much time to research any kinds of company shares variations, whether when their share prices will rise up of fall down in order to achieve buying the company's shares in the lowest price and selling the company's shares in the highest price level in order to earn profit.

Basic on this reason, they must need to spend much extra time to research share prices changing behavior every day, e.g. one working person will wait to leave his/her job, after he/she can spend time to gather data to research the day's share price changing behavior after dinner. So, the working person's right time may be his/her share price market research behavior. Before he/she may spend his/her night time to go to shopping after dinner, but nowadays, he/she will fogive to do his/her shopping behavior before dinner or after dinner at hight sometime. He/she will make decision to spend much night time to turn on computer to click on share market website to research his/her share purchase choice to investigate whether his/her share price whether it rises up or falls down at the moment in order to make his/her share buying or selling decision at ever night time.

I mean the when the country has many people are share investors, their shares investment behavioral spenging time which will influence many shops lose customers at might often because the country will have many people feel need to spend night time to turn on computer or watch television to investigate share price variation. So, the country will have many people / share investors choose to stay at home in order to carry on share price variation investigation behavior, they need to listen share market update news from radios or watch the share market update news from computer or TV at home every night. Consequenly, they must reduce times to leave themselves homes at night. So, their shopping behavior also will be reduced. Because these share investors feel need to spend time to investigate share price variation news at homes which can bring economic benefits (high opportunity benefits) when they choose to forgive to leave homes to go to shopping times (opportunity cost) every night.

On conclusion, it seems that when the country has many people are share investors, then their share price investigating behavior may bring negative shopping emotion at night. Consequently, the country's any one shop may lose many customers from this share investor consumer group in behavioral economic view. Hence, when the country's share investors number had been increasing rapidly, it will influence any shops lose many customers from this share investing customer group at night frequenly in short time, even long time in behavioral economic view, because their shopping desires or shopping emotion will be brought negative feeling when they make decisions to spend much time to listen radios or watch TV or computers share price update nes at night. Hence, share market will bring negative impact to influence consumer shopping desire or negative shopping emotion in behavioral economic view.

Can technology influence human shopping behavioral change?

Nowadays, technological development has reached mature stage, whether technological mature stage may bring positive or negative shopping emotion influence to global consumers. I shall aplly internet inventin or ecommerce shopping channel tool to explain whether internet technology can bring postive or negative influence to global consumer behavior in behavioral economic view.

Internet is a good technological tool, it brings e-commerce business chance. In fact, commonly, global has have many businessmen choose to use internet channel to carry on their products transactions between global online-buyers and their electronic websites. So, global many shoppers had begun to feel online shopping is more convenient to compare visiting shops shopping. Their shopping behaviors have been changed from internet technological tool. Global has many shoppers choose to buy any products from any overseas or local businessmen their web stores. They only need to spend time to find any businessmen their webstores to choose the most suitable products to pay visa to buy from their webstores. at homes. So, in general, global had have may shoppers had changed their shopping behaviors from visiting shops to visiting webstores at homes often.

So, it seems that internet technological tool had influenced global many shops disappear, but internet webstores will be replaced their actual shops on streets. Some of businessmen either they choose webstores to replace shops or choose websotes and shops both or still keep shops only. Hence, internet tool influences global businessmen have three kinds of products sale channels to let globa local and overseas consumers to choose how to buy their products.

However, in fact, many of global shoppers, youngers and olders had begun to accept to buy any products from webstores. They feel to spend time to leave homes to visit shops , their shopping behaviors will be wasted time to not essential part to their daily lives. Hence, since internet technological invention, it had changed many consumers their traditional visiting shops shopping habit to change to buying products from webstores channel.

However, on the one hand, internet creates webstores ecommerce shopping channel to let global many consumers do not need to leave homes to go to shopping. It brings negative visiting shops shopping emotion to global general consumers nowadays. But on the other hand, it also brings positive visiting internet webstores shopping emotion to global general consumer nowadays. So, it seems that global many consumers feel that they often do not need to spend much time to go out shopping. Many global consumers feel convenient and enjoy to choose any products to buy from different internet webstores, when the online buyer chooses the most suitable product, he she only needs to pay visa card to buy the product from the online seller's webstore conveniently at home.

Hence, online shopping can bring economic benefit to online buyers, e.g. avoiding walking time or spending transport fare to visit the shop to go to shopping, shortening or reducing shopping time to do another important matter.

On conclusion, global many consumers began feel online shopping can bring more economic benefits on shortening shopping time, avoiding transport fare spending aspect. So, online shopping will be popular shopping behavior for future long time. It may encourage global many shoppers can make rapid shopping decision in short time in order to carry on any products buying transaction to global any one online shopper in short time easily in behavioral economic view. So, global many businessmen had begun to build themselves one attraction webstore in order to persuade different countries consumers to choose to click themselves webstores from internet channel to buy any kinds of products in short time easily.

So, internet technology had changed consumers traditional shopping behaviors to build positive online shopping emotion as well as raise online sellers' any products sale chance easily in behavioral economic view.

Why and how human behavior may influence the country's economic growth or recession?

When one country has many people choose to do the same matter for one period, whether their behavior may influence the country's pvera; economic growth or recession . I shall attempt to indicate cases toexplain their relationship as below:

For flowing rubblish behavioral case example, do you feel that when the country has many people often flow rubblish on the streets, instead of their flowing rubblish behavior may bring streets dirty? But, their flowing rubblish behavior may explain that this country has people may have enough money to buy food to ear, or enough cloths to wear, enough bottles of water to drink, even they may have enough money to buy new television, radio, refrigeraters , washing machines, desktops or laptops electronic home products from old to new to use in order to satisfy their living needs. So, when they flow old electronic home products, their flowing old home electronic products behaviors may seem that they have enough money to buy other new home electronic products to replace old home electronic products to use at homes.

However, it seems thaat this country ought have many people have jobs to do. So, many of them, they can easy to make purchase decison to flow any old home electronic products and buy any new home electronic products to use . Because this country has many people have jobs to do. So, they can often not use old home electonic products to become rubblishs to flow on streets after they had bought any kinds of new home electronic homes.

In fact, it also implies that this country's economy grows rapidly. So, many businesses can glow up rapdly. When they expanded their businesses, they must need to increase employees number in order to let they help themselves to raise productivity or serve their clients absolutely. So, when the country has many businesses can grow up, it seems that its economy must be better or it is improved to compare past. Due to many different kinds of home electronic products had been often bought to use by this country people in this period. So, this country's any streets can be observed that expensive electronic home products were flowed on streets anywhere. then, this country will have many electronic home products sellers can sell their home electronic products very easily. When this country has many people can find any kinds of jobs to do easily. So, due to unemploymen rate had been decreasing.

In behavioral economic view, as this many electronic home products rubblish country case, we can observe this country may have many people have jobs to do. So, consumption number has been increased long time. So, cheap food, or expensive home electronic products may be rubblish on any streets. This country's people , their flowing rubblish behaviors may be explained that many of people have enough jobs to do, so they have ability to buy any good taste food to eat or buy any kinds of expensive electronic home products to use. So, this country's economy may be improved for this long period. So, in behavioral economic view, when this country can have many electronic home products rubblishs are flowed on anywherer in streets frequently. It seems that this country will have many people have jobs to do, so it causes they often change old home electronic products or replaced them easily, when they have enough income to spend to buy any kinds of new home electronic products to use at homes easily. Moreover, their flowing old electronic home products behaviors also indicate that this country has many people their salaries may be increased in possible from their emplyers. When this country can have many different kinds of home electornic products are sold. It means that this country's electronic home products needs or demand had been increasing, due to many people have jobs to do and income increases to excite their living of needs also improve. Consequently, this country may seem have better economic improvement. We can observe from this country's electronic home products rubblish increasing income in theis period.

On conclusion, this country ought experience economic growth at this period. So, " flowing expensive electronic home rubblish increasing number " may seem that this country's economic growth is rapidly in this period, due to many people have jobs to do as well as salaries increase in this period.

Technology how impacts human behavior changing?

Technology how influences human behavior to bring changing? For example, online share purchase and sale transaction from smart phone brings share investor can do share buying or selling transation in any where and any time conveniently, non manual driving auto vehicle, bring car owner feels comfortable and spends free time to do other matter, e.g. reading, listening mucis in himself or herself car freely. electrical energy vehicle can help car owner to reduce air polluton and it can brings the drivers do not feel drive long time in any journeys in order to avoid air pollution for environmental protection responsible car drivers in our societies. Thus, they will drive long time in any journeys when they can drive electronic energy cars to replace oil energy cars.

However, online technology can also bring consumers can choose to stay at homes to buy any things from seller individual online webstore conveniently. Such as online technology can bring shoppers do not need to spend much time to visit shops to buy any things. They can choose any kinds of products from any online sellers individual online webstores conveniently at homes. Online technology excite busy consumers can make purchase decision easily as well as it can help online sellers sell any kinds of products from internet easily.

In behavioral economic view, technology can change human behavior to be improved, it can let human feels comfortable, more free time ro use, rapid making any decisions, such as apply smart phones to make share purchase or sale transaction decision, online shopping decision, even travelling any where decision in short time, when the traveller finds the most cheap hotel accommodation room price and air ticket price frm any travel agent online tourism webstore, then the potential travel customer can follow the online hotel accommodation price and air ticket price data to make decision when to buy the air ticket from the airline travel agent or make decision when to prebook which hotel accommodation room to go to the country to travel from online travel agent tourism webstores. So, technology can encourage global any country travelers to make anywhere to trvel rapidly. If the traveler can find the country's general hotel rooms and airline tickets prices had been decreasing more sightly. The traveler may make travel decision to choose the country to travel in short time, then he/she can prebook the country;s any hotel room and airline ticket to pay by visa fraom the country's any hotel and airline travel agent webstores., before one week, even one month or more easily. Hence, online technology can also encourage traveler individual frequent travel times to be increased, due to global travelers can find any hotel rooms and airline tickets prices from internet conveniently at homes. They do not need to spend time to visit any airline travel agent to enquire travel choice country's hotel rooms prices and airline ticket prices. They can compare global travel of countries choices ' all hotels rooms and airline agents air tickets prices to make prebook airline seat and hotel room decision before one week, one month even six months early.

On conclusion, online technology can encourage global travelers can make travelling any where and when traveling time desicions easily. It can excite tourism industry develops in long time. Also, such as electricity cars invention can encourage environment protection car owners do car purchase decision easily, because they can choose to drive electronic energy cars to replace oil energy cars in order to avoid air pollution occurs easily. So, electronic cars can increase electronic car purchasrs number, due to many of environmental protection attitude of car owners can choose to drive electricity cars to bring air cleans, even non -manual driving cars can encourage lazy driving and free time driving car owners to choose to buy non-manual (artificial intelligent) cars to drive , because they can spend much free time to read, listen music or do any matters in themselves cars, they do not need to drive cars, robotic (AI) auto driving machine is such one non-manual driver to help them to drive themselves cars confidently. So, non-manual driving cars can attract lazy and enjoying free time driving car owners to choose to buy to replace traditional manual cars to drive easily. Moreover, online share transaction can help any share investors to make share buying and selling decision in short time easily. When they can apply smart phones technological tool to carry on share buying and selling activities easily. They can observe any share rising or falling price suitation from smart phones in any where any any time easily. So, smart phone technology can help global any shareholders to make share purchase and sale transaction easily. So, technology can encourage human makes decision in short time rapidly.

How and why employees behaviors may influence economy development?

In behavioral economy view,I believe the country's any organizational employees behavior may bring indirect relationship to influence the country's long term economic development. I shall indicate past manufacture industry social development period to explain their relationship. For many countries' past business activities had belonged to manufacturing industry, such as US, UK past before 1980 year, it focused on steel manufacturing and steel manufacturing related machine products. So, US, Uk developed countries manufacturing industries may be past main country's economic income sources. I assume US , UK past had one million number different kinds of industries. They ought had about seven houndred thousand number organizational businesses were belonged to manufactured industry. They may include:

Steel manufacturing and steel related machine manufacturing, e.g. vehicle manufacturing, home appliances, e.g. washing machine, television, radio, refrigerate cooler, heater, air condition etc. different kinds of different kinds of steel -related manufacturing machine, they were manufactured from US, UK steel machine manufacturers. So, US, Uk the other three hundred thousand number industry may be general service industry, e.g. hotel service, restaurent, cinema, public transport service, tourism lesiure , wine bar, supermarket etc. different kinds of non-manufacturing industries business organizations were operated in UK, US past before 1980 year.

So, in UK, US developed countries industry development history, they ought have high percentage of businesses belonged to steel related manufacturing machine and steel products. Also, in the past before 1980 year, US, Uk business employers , they employed many workers are manufacturing workers. They needed to spend long time to work in factories. They were skillful workers, and they are trained to manufacturing cars, washing machine, television, heater, etc. even steel itself different kinds of steel related products to prepare to deliver to their shops to sell to US, Uk local or overseas clients.

So, I believe that past UK, US ought employ many employees, they belonged to skillful manufacturing workers, manufacture increasing steel machine or steel related machine number of products rapidly daily. So, if UK, US had had many of these manufacturing factories owned high skillful workers, then their manufacturing steel-related machine or steel both kinds of products number must be influenced to raise rapidly. Consequently, their steel machine manufacturing products would been exported to overseas or would been sold to local both markets , they may be influenced to raise sale number. They (these manufacturing workers) needed to be trained to know how to manufactur these different kinds of machine products in the efficient teams and they ought to be trained to raise their efficiencies in order to shorten time to manufacturing many kinds of steel related manufacturing machine or steel itself products rapidly. So , if their efficiencies and manufacturing performance was improved, these US, UK any one manufacturing worker and their teams ought achieve raising productivities significantly.

Hence, when past UK, US manufacturing industry development period, if these two countries' any manufacturing factories could have many manufacturing workers could be trained to be skillful and proficient manufacturing workers. Then, in past every day to these factories workers, they ought help their steel or steel related manufacturing employers to raise any kinds of machine or steel products number in every team. So, when past in the manufacturing industry development, US, UK could have many factories' manufacturing workers themselves steel or steel related machine products manufacturing skill could be trained to to improve to any kinds of these machine or steel manufacuring products quality as well as their products number could be influenced to raise by themselves skillful improvement significantly every day.

Then, what would be influenced to occur to past UK, US manufacturing industry period? In behavioral economic view, when these two manufacturing industry developed countries, such as UK, US , if they had many factories workers can be trained to improve their skill in order to achieve any kinds of steel or steel-related machine products quality could be improved as well as products manufacturing number could be also increased absolutely.

In consequence, past UK and US both countries ought increase themselves any kinds of steel and steel related machine products number to be supplied to themselves local shops to let local clients to choose any one kind of machine manufacturing products to buy easily as well as they could also export to supply overseas any countries to buy their different kinds of steel or steel related machine products to let overseas steel or steel related manufacturing machine product buyers, they can have many of these different kinds of these steel or steel-related different kinds of manufacturing machine from UK and UK these both countries easily to compare other countries.

On conclusion, I believe that past US, and UK macro manufacturing industry income GDP would increase significantly. So, they would have good economic growth performance because when many of these manufacturing workers themselves manufacturing effort could be improved. So, it explained when employees manufacturing abilities can influence economic growth indirectly.

Robots invention whether they can help organizations to raise efficiencies or inefficiencies?

In behavioral economic view, in any organizations, when the organization hopes its worker teams can raise efficiencies , the organization may choose to increase more workers number and/or it can provide training to improve these workets themselves skills in order to raise their efficiencies. For one warehouse example, when the warehouse increases many goods , they are needed to delivered these goods from the shelves to the delivering destination locations. If this warehouse supervisors feel these workers themselves goods delivery speeds are slow, which is possible due to this warehouse's workers number is not enough. So, this warehouse supervisor ought increase workers number in order to increase their goods delivery speed in order to deliver goods from the shelves to every indicated goods delivery destination in order to let any one lorry driver can transport the right kinds of goods and ensure the accurate goods number to transport to any one client home rapidly.

However, if this warehouse supervisor planed to buy several warehouse goods delivery robots to assist these warehouse workers to find the right kinds of goods from shelves and then deliver to the right destination location in the warehouse. So, these warehouse orkers can concentrate on counting the accurate goods number and ensuring the right kinds of goods in order to prepare to let lorry drivers to transport these goods to these goods of buyers themselvers homes rapidly. Consequently, in the first step, robots can concentrate on finding th right goods from shelves and delivers them to the right goods transportation of location destination. Then, in the second step, these warehouse workers can concentrate on counting the accurate goods number and ensuring the right kinds of goods in order to prepare to put them to the lorry. Consequently, when warehouse robots and warehouse workers can cooperate to work together, the most important, robots, can deal on finding the right kinds of goods and deal on delivering the accurate number of goods of job duty as well as these warehouse workers can only concentrte on counting the right kinds of goods number in order to avoid it has none any mistake of wrong kinds of goods and inaccurate goods of delivery number to be transported to the lorry and to deliver to any one buyer's home.

So, it seems that warehouse robots ought help any one warehouse worker to raise himself efficiency and avoid goods delivery of mistake occurrence easily as well as their help to warehouse workers that can let any one goods buyer feels their goods can be delivered to their homes rapidly. Moreover, warehouse robots can also help these warehouse workers to raise efficiencies because warehouse robots can help them to shorten goods delivery time between any one shelf and any one goods delivery destination of location in the warehuse because robots may help them to find the right kinds of goods from the right shelf in the short time. So, any one worker does not need to spend long time to seek anywhere is the right shelf location for the kind of goods when the kind of goods are needed to deliver to the buyer's home from lorry. Warehouse robots can help them to do this aspect of " finding the goods from the right shelf in short time job duty". So, any one warehouse worker only needed tospend less time to do the counting of any right kind of goods number and ensuring the right kind of goods job duty. Consequently, this warehouse 's any one worker, his any one kind of goods delivery time may be reduced, because robots' assistance and they may have more confidence to avoid mistake to deliver the wrong number of goods and/or the wrong kind of goods to any one goods buyer's home.

On conclusion, it seems that warehouse robots ought may help any one warehouse worker to raise efficiency for any one team in the warehouse as well as the warehouse any one supervisor does not need to spend much time to observe any one worker individual performance for " goods delivery job duty aspect" because their goods delivery job duty that had been replaced to do by these several warehouse robots. Robots can achieve the more accurate of right kinds of goods and the right number of goods delviery job performance to compare any one of human warehouse worker themselves right kinds of goods of delivery and right number of goods of delivery job performance. So, when robots can participate to cooperate with this warehouse's any one worker to do their goods of delivery job duty in this warehouse every day. Then, robots can raies any one of supervisor individual confidence in order to let they do not need to spend time to observe any one of worker individual whose goods of delivery job performane. They can concentrate on supervising any one worker whose goods transport to lorry in the final step in order to avoid to deliver wrong goods number and / or wrong kind of goods to any one goods buyer's home every day. Consequently, this warehouse's overall teams of their delviery of goods performance many be improved by robotss' participatin to goods of delivery task as well as this warehouse's oveall teams themselves efficiencies may be influenced to raise by robots' goods of delivery task participation.

Why social behavior may influence organizational strategy needs to be changed ?

Why any organizations need to know whether nowadays social behaivor how has been changing in order to implement the kind of the most right strategy to achieve the profit aim pursue in possible. I shall indicate nowadays ecommerce or online, customer shopping behavior to explain above question concerns they ought have close relationship between social behavior and organizational strategic choice or organizational behavioral changing need.

On nowadays ecommerce business, or online shopping model, this kind of shopping model in global many young and old age consumers like to apply internet tool to choose any country sellers website stores in order to stay at home to buy any kinds of products from themselves webstores in global societies.

In fact, online shopping model had been popular for long time above to twenty years. Most of global sellers will make decision to design themselves webstores in order to attract global many online buyers to choose to buy their products from themselves webstores. So, it seems that social consumers purchase behaviors had been changed to online shopping from internet invention.

Hence, social consumers purchase behavioral changes may influence any organizations' strategies need to be changed from visiting shops purchase strategy model to online purchase strategy model, if the seller still concentrate on concentrate on considerate how to design itelf , but neglects to considerate how to design itself webstore, e.g. how to design attract product photos to put on itself webstore, how to arrange sale price information location to be putted on webstore and visa card payment location on itself webstore in order to let any one online buyer can feel very easier to buy itself any kinds of products from itself webstore. Then, its potential online buyers will be influenced to increase number when they can find this online seller itself any kinds of products photes and every kinds of product sale price information and visa card payment channel locations easily from itself webstore.

So, it implies that nowadays any one seller ought need to design one webstore to let any one online overseas and domestic consumers can have chance to click itself webstore to choose any one kind of product to buy conveniently when he/she does not hope to leave him/her home to go to shop, because nowadays social shopping behaviors had been influenced to change when internet invention, them it gives another online purchase method to replace visiting shops purchase method to global any one buyer in nowadays societies.

So, if nowadays any one seller still concentrate on how to design itself shop display in order to put any kinds of product on shelf in order to let any one visiting shop customer to find the kind of product to buy, but it neglects to change to choose to pursue another new technological shopping method, such as webstore purchase method in order to implement effective strategy to design the most right webstore as well as in order to attract global overseas and local consumers to find itself webstore easily from website and find its any one kind of product phots and sale price and visa card payment button in order to choose to buy itself any kinds of products in the short time. Consequently I believe that the seller will lose many customers from overseas and local when its other same or similar product sellers choose to design themselves webstores in order to let global any one product buyer can buy themselves any one kind of product when they can pay visa card to buy their products from them webstores conveniently when they stay at home habitly. Then, the seller will lose many global potential customers in long time.

On conclusion, in behavioral economic view, any consumer behavioral social changing, which will influence any in order to avoid customers number loses significantly . In future time, organizations need to make rapid decision in order to implement the most reasonable and the most useful strategy in order to avoid global potential customers number reduces or lose them in long time. So, social behavioral changing environment ought influence any global organizations need to decide how to change themselves strategies in order to avoid customers loses significantly in future time.

How and why human behavior may influence economic growth or recession?

May ourselves daily behaviors influence our global societial continue economic growth or recession? Do they have cause and effect close relationship between human behaviors and global economic growth or recession? I shall apply behavioral economic theory to analyze and explain whether ourselves daily behaviors and our global societial economic growth or recession which have close cause and effect relationship as below:

Every country itself economic development must depend on any business activities, otherwise, any kinds of business activities must need ourselves business activities or behaviors in order to achieve any business activities as well as achieve the country's overall economic development in macro view. However, any country's overall business activites or behaviors which must depend on any kinds of individual businessmen, themselves employees daily working behavior or activity or performance in order to help them to attract or increase many clients number to acieve " earning profit" aim. So, it seems that any individual business, itself overall every department individual working behavior is one main factor to influence the company's overall business performance.

For agricultural fruit and meat food farming industry example, such as New Zealand is a farming main target industry country. It had had many New Zealanders were daily themselves own farming businesses for many years. Their farming businesses include growing fruit, sheep, cow, pig pork, meat etc. food sale business. If the New Zealand farmer owned a large size farming land, then he will choose either growing fruit or feeding sheeps, pigs, cows to be meat to to transport to New Zealand supermarkets to help them to sell to their farmers meet to New Zealanders in order to earn profit. Thus, if the New Zealand farmer owned large size of farming lands, then he needs to employ many farming employees (farming workers) to help him to carry on farming business daily tasks, e.g. picking up friuts, feeding pigs, cows, sheeps to eat food daily. These daily farming jobs are very important to influence this New Zealand farmer's meats or fruits sale number whether they can be easy or diffcult to sell in New Zealand supermarkets , if these farming workers can own encough farming knowledge or skill to know how to pick up fruits method and make judgement to know whether it is right time to pick up the kind of fruits from the trees , as well as know how feed this pigs, sheeps, cows to eat food in order to let they are better health. Consequently, their farming behaviors which can let these animals can provide the best taste and enough meat from these animals to let New Zealander to buy to eat from New Zealand any one supermarket. Even these New Zealand farming workers can know whether the kinds of fruits, e.g. oranges, apples, gapes etc. fruits whether they ought be picked up from the trees at the right time. Consequently, they can make judgement to decide to pick up any kinds of the best taste fruits to let any one New Zealander to buy to eat from any one supermarket in New Zealand. Otherwise, if they do not make judegement to know whether the kind of fruit ought not be picked up because they still need longer time to continue grow up to increase fruit size and better taste from the trees in order to let any one fruit buyer can feel better taste when they eat this kind of fruit later. If they can buy this kind of fruit to eat later, then this New Zealand farmer's his fruit buyers can buy the best taste of this kind of fruit to eat from an yone supermarket in New Zealand. Consequently, many New Zealand supermarkets will choose to buy any kinds of fruits from this farmer fruit supplier when they feel this farmer's fruits can provide more better taste fruits to compare other farmers' fruits.

Thus, due to New Zealand is one farming main income source country. It's any kinds of fruits and meats need to be export to overseas to sell , instead of local sale. It's GDP percent is very high to whole country 's overall income source. So, any one New Zealand farmer individual and any one farming worker individual working behavior will influence its economy whether it is influenced to grow or recession possible. Moreover, it also seems that farming workers' farming knowledge and skill will influence themselves farming daily activities to achieve the aim of the number of increase or decrease to any kinds of fruits whether they are better taste or the number of increase of decrease to any kinds of meats whether they are better taste to supply to any one New Zealand fruit or meat buyers to eat from any one New Zealand supermarket. So, it implies that any one New Zealand farming worker individual farming behavior may influence any kinds of fruits or any kinds of meat taste because they are transported to any one supermarket to sell in New Zealand.

Consequently, if New Zealans had many farmers can teach god farming knowledge and skill to let their any one farming workers know how to decide judgement to decide when it is right time to pick up any kinds of fruits from trees , or how to grow them on soil in order to let they can grow rapidly. Then, many different kinds of fruits can be provided to let any one New Zealanders can eat the best taste of fruits when their fruits are supplied to any one New Zealand supermarkets. Even, if they knew how to feed foods to pigs, cows, sheeps to eat daily. Then they can be more health and they can provide the best taste of meats to let any one New Zealanders can buy their meats from any one New Zealand supermarkets. Moreover, their fruits and meats can be transported to overseas to let any one country fruits or meats buyers can choose any kinds of New Zealand meats and fruits to buy to eat from themselves countries supermarkets. Then, many overseas fruit and meat buyers will perfer to choose New Zealand any kinds of fruits or meats to buy to compare other countries fruits or meats to buy when they go to any one local supermarkets.

On conclusion, it seems that New Zealand farming workers themselves farming behavior may influence their farming employers any kinds of fruits or meats sale number and income because their farming task behaviors must influence whether their fruits or meats taste are the better taste or worse taste to compare their other local farmers (the farmer competitors) whose fruits or meats taste. If tthe farmer's any one farming worker can be trained to learn how to know to feed animals skill and when is the most right time to pick up any kinds of fruits from trees or how to grow them on the soil methods. Due to these farming worker individual farming behavior may influence his different finds of fruits and meats sale number to be increase or decrease, so these any one New Zealand farmer must need to depend on any one farming worker whose farming working methods, if their farming working behaviors can be the best to influence any kinds of fruits to grow rapid or any kinds of pigs, cows, sheeps animals grow up rapidly , then their sale number may be increase significantly and their taste can be improved to let any New Zealand or overseas meat or fruit buyer to buy to eat to feel from any one New Zealand or overseas supermarkets, then New Zealand's agriculture industry must be influenced to increase. In the world, any one fruit or meat buyer must choose to buy New Zealand's fruit and meat to eat in prefer to compare other countries' fruits and meats. So, New Zealand's GDP may be influenced to raise from any one New Zealand farming worker individual farming working behaviors.

Reasons why human behavior may influence economic recession or growth?

Can ourselves daily behaviors or activies influence ourselves countries' economic growth or recession? I shall attempt to explain the reasons why they have direct or indirect relationship between human behavior and economy growth or recession as below:

I shall indicate environment pollution case to attempt to explain above question. Our societies had been experiencing servious environment pollution challenge. However, environment pollution , such as air pollution is caused by air planes and vehicles emission by air planes and vehicles emission as well as water pollution is caused by plastic rubblish, or dirty water or oil or gas chemical material, these both kinds of pollution ought may bring economic recession and this both kinds of pollution are caused by human ourselves daily foolish activities.

I believe human behavior and economy and pollution which have cause and effect relationship. I shall analyze this environment pollution case to explain why they have case and effect relationship between human foolish behavior and environment pollution and economic recession as below:

When global societies had many people like to buy cars to drive to bring emission to fresh air on the roads as well as many manufacturing factories will bring emission to pollute fresh air in their manufacturing processes. Factories and cars will bring air pollution , due to factories need to pollute fresh air in order to manufacture many products and car owners need to drive their cars to go to offices or leisure places. Their cars will also bring emisson to pollute fresh air. On consequence, car owners themselves frequent driving behaviors and factory workers themselves frequent manufacturing behaviors may bring environment pollution. Technology or human behavior whether may influence economic growth or recession. Moreover, air planes also brings emission to pollute air when they are flying in sky. Also, when ships bring oil pollution or sea plastic rubblishs bring pollution to global oceans.

In fact, manufactuers and cars owners, such as factories workers manufacturing behaviours ans car owners driving behaviors and pilots driving air planes flying behaviors and ships transport behaviors, which may cause plastic rubblish, oil or gas emission to sky or sea or on the road to cause ocean and air pollution is serious. However, human ourselves need to buy cars to drive to satisfy ourselves driving leisure or enjoyment, travelers need to catch air planes to travel to enjoy leisure needs, factories workers need help factories to manufacture many products to sell to customers to satisfy their using needs. oil exploration needs to find lands to explore new oil lands.

All of these business and leisure activites may bring serious air and water pollution. However, due to serious air and water pollution will bring earth warming challenge , such as some countries temperature will be influences to rise up to 40 degree or higher br earth warming. However, earth warming is caused by air and ocean pollution. Pollution must be caused by human ourselves, driving cars leisure and factories manufacturing business activities. Hence, if human decided to continue to do these foolish behaviors, we only pursue to manufacture different kinds of industrial products or drive cars to enjoy leisure aims, but we also neglect ourselves behaviors may bring environment pollution. Then, earth warming or earth temperature will be influenced to rise up absolutely in long term. Moreover, if our future earth will be influenced to bring serious high temperature effect by human ourselves these foolish behaviors.

On consequencey, warth warming will bring serious economic losses in possible because when ourselves earth temperature had been influenced to rise up to 40 degree or high. Ourselves health will be caused poor, due to we will feel difficult breath, we must need often tried and hard to work, due to our nervous and health will be influenced to poor by pollution and earth warming effect. Also, we need to pay more money to see doctors when we had long life. Then, our societies will lose may strong labors to help manufacturers to work, e.g. factories will reduce workers number to help manufacturers to produce more different kinds of products, due to workers health is general poor. Due to lacking enough workers to manufacture products, our societies will begin to reduce enough supply number of products to sell to global consumers to satisfy their use needs.

On conclusion, in behaviroal economic view, our societies will lose many labors due to their bodies are not health by air and water pollution. Global economic and business activities will be influenced to worse by global workers reducing number reason. So, economic recession will begin to occur in possible when pollution reaches the serious level.

How employee behavior influences organizational development?

Can any organizational department employee individual behavior may help the organization to bring long term development? When one employee individual behavior, manager won't feel whose task behavior may help organizational development, but when the department has many teams cooperate to work together , all of these team employees whose task behaviors may help their organization to bring long term development.

I shall explain how any why when the organization has many departments, as well as when every team memmber individual behavior may help whole organization to bring long term development in possible as below:

Every organization must need efficient departent to cooperate to work together. They may include human resource, finance, logistic, facility management, sales, marketing , operateional , warehouse , factory manufacture , research and development, purchase, customer service etc. different kinds of departments to cooperate to work together. So, any one employee individual behavior, include manager, leader, supervisor, worker, salesperson, manufacture worker, adminisration staff, factory or logistic worker etc. themselves task behavior whether his/her performance is worse or better , whose task behavior ought bring long term good or bad influence to cause the organization's whose efficiency, or performance , whether it can be influenced to improve significantly. For car factory manufacture workers department example, it exmploys 100 car manufacturing workers. They need to manufacture at least 50 cars in order to bring enough car manufacture number to supply to global car buyers to choose to buy (satisfaction to car buyers their driving leisure activity needs). However, if this car manufacture firm employs many low skilful car manufacture workers, their inefficient car skill may bring cars manufacture number reduces, they can not achieve to reach the at least 50 cars manufacture number, if these 100 car manufacture workers. They have half number of workers, they only manufacture 30 to 40 cars number at least daily. So, it seems that this car manufacture firm will have half car manufacture workers bring the low cars manufacture number to compare the another half cars manufacture workers, when this proficient car manufacture workers may manufacture at least 60 or more cars manufacture number daily. So, it explains that this inefficient car manufacture workers will not help this car manufacture company to manufacture enough cars number in order to supply to global car market to sell to satisfy global car buyers needs, when car buyers demand number is more thn car manufacture supply number in supply and demand view. Hence, in long term, if this car manufacture company can not employ new proficient car manufacture workers to replace those inefficient or low skillful car workers. Consequently, its car manufacture number must be influenced to reduce and it can not satisfy global car buyers driving leisure needs.

However, if this car manufacture firm also has shop to sell itself any kinds of cars, instead of manufacturing cars product. So, it needs have both main departments to help it to earn profit. The first step, it needs have proficient car manufacture workers to help it to manufacture at least 50 cars from every car worker in order to have enough cars number to be provided to global car sellers to help it to sell to global car customers. Second step, if it decided to attempt to sell itself cars. Then, it needs to set up car shops in global to different countries in order to let global car buyers may visit its global any one car shop to enquire any one car etc. salesperson about any car quality, speed, gas useful, price, safety, etc. information questions and they can attempt to sit in any one car to feel whether which car can let them to feel more comfortable to make final car purchase decision in any one shop. So, if this car company can provide good sale speaking skillful training to any one car salesperson to let his/her to know whether how to explain every kind of car function and feature, manufacture method etc. questions, then I believe that they can influence any one car buyer to makecar purchase choice decision more easily. So, it this car manufacturer hopes it may attempt to earn profit from different countries car sellers and car buyers both. It ought also provide training course to all general car salespeople to be proficient owning sale speaking skillful professional skill in order to prepare having more confidence to persuade any one car customer to make car purchase choice from any one car salesperson more easily to compare global other car sellers.

Hence, if this car manufacturer could build both car manufacturing team and car sale team more proficient. However, if this car manufacturer hopes to develop itself car manufacture busness to expend to car sale business both in success. It must need to spend long term to provide training courses to general car manufacture workers and general car salespeople both to be proficient car skillful manufacture workers and proficient car skillful salespeople in order to help they can manufacture enough car numbers and help they can persuade may car customers can make car purchase decision in short time when they visit its any one car shop.

However, this car manufacture company explains why every car manufacture worker whose manufacturing behavior and every car salesperson sale persuading speaking ability may help this car manufacture company to expand from its car manufacture market to car sale market development in sussess in possible. So, this car manufacture firm must need these two kinds of essential human resource elements in order to achieve its cars sale number and cars manufacture number increasing aim. They may include proficient car manufacture workers and proficient car salespeople both human resource elements. These both human resource daily task behavior may influence its long term task efficient performance in order to expand itself car sale business in success from itself car manufacture business easily. If it hopes to expand its car manufacture business to car sale business in success. It must need to provide training to these two departments general staffs to be proficient staffs in order to supply enough cars number to its global car shops to let global car buyers can choose its any kinds of cars to buy in any time.

Morevoer, if this car manufacture company can have good skillful of car research and development department , it aims to research and innovate any new technological cars invention in order to improve its any traditional old kinds of cars to be innovative new kinds of cars from every year. Consequently, its any new innovative cars ought attract global any one car buyer to make car purchase choice final decision more easily, because its any kinds of manufacturng cars can be innovated rapidly to compare its any one car manufacturing competitors, when its nay kinds of cars can be shorten time to innovate within three months, but its any one car manufacturing competitors need to spend more than three months, even one year to innovate themselves traditional old cars products in long term. Hence, its car staffs research and development department staffs must need own good car product design ability, proficient car engineering knowledge , even car invention knowledge in order to innovate its any one kind of car product in short time and introduce to let its global car proficient car buyers feel surprise to its any one kind of innovative car products to compare its any one car manufacturer.Hence, these four departments: car manufacture, car sale and car research and development anr car training departments must need concentrate resource to provide enough training to any one staffs in order to achieve the best performance.

On conclusion, all these departments staffs their performance can influence car manufacture aim to chance to car manufacture and sale aim more significantly. it explains why some main department staffs whole behaviors may influence any organizational performance significantly.

Artificial intelligent Human clever and art creating ability methods

How robots create human clever and art creating ability? Nowadays robots invention may help businesses to reduce employees number, improve performance, raise productivities, reduce cost in service industry,manufacturing industry, office , warehouse, restaurant, hotel , factory, cinema etc. different kinds of business environments, even public transport tools. However, instead of robots may bring these above advantages to any kinds of business working and service environments, whether robots may also help human to create clever and image creating ability. I shall attempt to answer this question:

On the one hand, I believe that past technology ,e.g. machine , it should not have ability to help human to create clever and image creative ability,but nowadays, robots invention that I believe it had had enough ability to help future human to raise more clever and more creating image or painting picture, art design etr. image ability, after robots had been experienced above more than ten years improvement stage from early research stage to invention stage, till to nowadays improvement stage, e.g. non-manual driving auto vehicels, even future non-manual driving skill may be improved to apply to public transport tools, e.g. trams, trains,buses, airplanes, ships etc. public transport tools, when non-manual driving skills can be improved to own the most safe driving skillful ability to compare human driving skills.

On another hand, when robots could be invented to be applied to medical or hospital surgery aspect, e.g. roboting surgerys may help surgery doctors to do complex surgery in surgery rooms, or serving patients tasks in any hospital working environments. They can help nurses and doctors to spend more time to do more important tasks urgently, so medical or surgery serving robots may help nurses and surgery doctors to reduce task load pressure and create clever or improve their surgery skills to when they can cooperate to work in hospitals.

On the other hand, robots can be invented to help any public transport drivers to avoid more traffic accidents occurrence on any countries roads. So, it seems that non-manual driving public transport tools invention may also help human drivers to improve driving skills in possible, when they can learn how to avoid sudden traffic accidents occurrence in any countries roads in any time. so, any kindsof public transport tool drivers ought learn how to avoid traffic accidents skills from future non-manual driving robots invention. Instead of non-manual driving robots and hospital patients medical care or surgery service robots may help public transport tools drivers and hospital nurses and doctors to concentrate on spending time to treat any more important and urgent matters every days. Even, future restaurants may let cooking restaurants may let cooking robots to help human cookers to cook more different kinds of good taste food, to human cookers may learn cooking robots cooking skills in order to improve themselves traditional cooking skills often, in order to compare their cooking skills between human cookers and cooking robots.

On conclusion, it seems that cooking robots ought help human cookers to create any kinds of new cooking skills. Moremove, futuer robot cookers ought be future human cookers their cooking coaches. These robot cookers will help human cookers to create clever cooking skills in possible. Also, future non-manual driving robots ought help human drivers to create new driving skills in order to improve their driving skills to reduce sudden traffic accidents occurrence easily on any countries roads in any time, future hospital surgery or patient care service robots may help surgeons or nurses to do any surgerys in surgery rooms or looking care patients in hospitals. So, when robot surgeons help human surgeons to do complex surgerys in surgerical rooms, human surgeons can learn how to do more complex surgerical tasks for every surgeons when human surgeons can observate every surgerical robots how to do surgeons together. Hence, it seems that robot surgeons also may create future human surgeons themselves innovate surgerical skills from traditional surgerical skills improvement. So, future artificial intelligent technology ought help any kinds of human occupations to create clever, even improvement themselves traditional skills to new innovative skills absolutely.

Why does technology raise online products sale demand and reduces shops products sale demand?

Nowadays robot technology is popular to be applied to different aspects of our daily lives. They may include: non-manual driving vehicles, smart phones, space rockets, kitchen cookers, shopping centres service, cinema ticket sale, etc. different kinds of businesses demand. However, instead of internet invention may influence global communication, media channel is changed to computer internet, media channel is changed to computer internet, media communication from traditional newspaper, letter, TV, radio etc. communication channel. So, any internet users may click to yahoo.com news website to read global news from computer yahoo.com website easily.

In fact, internet technology is also used from businesses. They attempt to set up themselves web stores to sell their products from themselves webstores. So, any one product buyers may buy any kinds of products from any one webstores when they stay at homes. It is very convenient and common to future any one webstore shoppers. It brings this question: Can webstores help online product purchases needs raise and influence shop product purchases need reduce?

In demand and supply view, when one product price raises, its sale demand ought reduce, unless, it can attract to influence customers need consideration or its supply number decreases. But, when one product is increasing sale price to seel from the seller's webstore, whether its sale number will be influenced to reduce. Also, when the kind of product is selling and its sale price is raised, whether it can still keep demand number increase as well as whether it can influence its similar kinds of competitor their products sale demand number to reduce from shop sale channel.

In demand and supply view, when one product price raises, its sale demand ought reduce, unless, it can attract to influence customers need consideration or its supply number decreases. But when one product is increasing sale price to sell from the seller's webstore, whether its sale number will be influenced to reduce. Also, when the kind of product is selling and its sale price is raised, whether it can still keep demand number increases as well as whether it can influence its similar kinds of competitors their products sale demand number to reduce from shop sale channel.

I suppose that webstore sale may influence shop sale demand number decreases, because when internet is popular to use, when one country's buyer wants to buy one kind of product, but he/she can not find the kind of product can be bought from himself/herself home country. If he/she can findthe kind of product to buy from any one of overseas webstore from internet channel at home in any time. Then, he/she will be influenced to make purchase decision from the seller's websote immediately. So, it implies that when on consumer plans to buy one kind of product, he / she will attempt to find the kind of product from any one seller's webstore in preferat home, if he/she spend long time to find the kind of product from many of webstores, but he /she still does not find the kind of product from many of webstores, then he/she will choose to visit any one shop to attempt to buy the kind of product.Hence, online shopping purchase channel will be prefer choice to compare visiting shopd purchase channel in nowadays society.

So, it explains that why the kind of product online sale number may influence the kind of similar product visiting shop sale number either increases or decreases. It means that the kind of product visiting shops sale number may still increases , if the kind of similar products supply number is not enough , they are difficult to let any one online buyer to find to buy from any one webstore. Otherwise, if the kind of similar products sale supply number is enough to let any one online buyer to find from many webstores. Then, they can influence the similar kinds of shop products purchase demand to reduce and their shops purchase demand will be also influenced to reduce from webstores purchase channel.

On conclusion, it explains that the kind of shop products demand number ought be influenced to increase or decrease, when the similar kind of products can be bought easily from many webstores from internet (ecommerce) shopping channel. Internet (online) technology may help the seller to raise the kind of product competitive ability on purchase demand aspect, when there are not many other sellers can provide webstores to sell the similar kind of products and they only concentrate on selling the kind of similar products from shops to let any one online buyer to frind from may webstores. Then, they can influence the similar kinds of shop products purchase demand to reduce and their shops purchase demand will be also influenced to reduce from webstores purchase channel. Hence, webstore and shop both purchase channel explains that the similar kinds of shop products demand number will be influenced to increase or decrease , when the kinds of product can be bought easily from many webstores from internet shopping channel. Internet technology may help the seller to raise the kind of product competitive abilty to raise purchase demand when there are not many other sellers can provide webstores to sell the kind of similar products and they only concentrate on selling the kind of similar products from shops.

Does car technological development reach mature stage to help economic development?

Our societies had been developing too many years. In our past technological aspect, machine invention had began till to computer invention till to internet invention. It seems that our technological development stage may reach mature stage. Why do I feel our technological development had reached mature stage. I shall apply demand and supply economic theory to explain this question as below:

I shall indicate car development industry to explain whether when car development stage can reach mature stage, it may help global economic growth. In our car technological development stage, it is from gas energy car invention till to nowadays battery energy car invention till to even future non-manual driving car invention. Do you feel that when human (car buyers) felt environmental protecion need to avoid air pollution. So, battery energy cars demand number may increase , it will influence gas energy cars demand number reduces. Even, if future non0manula driving cars invention succeed, lazy driving car buyers will choose to buy non-manual driving (robot driving cars) in preference. So, it is possible that , it will influence future gas energy cars demand number reduces much. I mean that when car buyers can choose many different kinds of non-manual driving cars and battery energy cars to buy. Then, gas energy cars demand number must be influenced to reduce very much as well as gas energy cars supply number will be influenced to reduce to avoid sale prices reduce.

Hence, it explains why future car technological development will reach mature stage when both kinds of non-manual driving cars and battery energy cars are invented to the mature stage. When these two kinds of cars invention can satisfy future global car buyers driving needs. Then, car maufacturers won't need to spend too much time to continue to attempt to invent any new kinds of cars in order to excite future car buyers' purchase decision. So, I believe that car technological development will reach mature stage within five years, if non-manual driving cars and battery energy cars are invented in success and they can be popular to accept to drive to global car buyers.

On conclusion, when car technological development reaches matural stage, it will help future economy continue grows because when car manufacturers had invented many new kinds of non-manual driving cars and new kinds of non-manual driving cars and new battery energy car sale market. Then, they will encourage or attract global many car buyers choose to buy these both kinds of cars products in preference to compare to traditional gas energy car products. So, they will influence many traditional gas- energy car buyers forgive to drive gas energy cars to avoid non pollution and lazy driving behavioral feeling. So, gas energy car reselling number will increase between gas energy car drivers and past non-owning any car buyers. Also, non-manual driving cars and battery energy car supplying number will be influenced to increase when battery energy car buyers and non-manual driving car buyers driving needs increase.

Consequently, these factors will influence global gas energy cars, non-manual driving cars and battery energy cars their cars purchase and sale transactions increase in future global car market. So, I believe that global car technological development could reach matural stage, then it will infuence global car buyers number increases as well as this car technological mature development stage may also bring global rapid economic growth future non-manual driving car buyers and battery energy car buyers both number increases.